# Python codes to fetch & analyze NSE stock market data

Dr. M. Kanagasabapathy
Dr. R. Vishnushankar
Dr. R. Jaganath
Rajapalayam Rajus' College
Rajapalayam 626117
Tamil Nadu, India

**ISBN:** 978-93-341-5194-7
**Edition:** I
**Published on:** 26th October 2024
**Format:** Paperback

# Preface

This book gives a gentle introduction and basics on how to use Python to fetch and to analyze the live stock market data for NSE listed stocks and indices. It has the compilation of Python codes to procure and to evaluate, several historical data for equities as well as indices such as NIFTY and Bank NIFTY. Algorithms to get the haircut data for stocks and mutual funds are also incorporated.

Despite these, codes are encompassed to acquire and to scrutinize the NSE live market data for option chain of indices and equities that are listed in NSE followed by saving the data as .csv spreadsheets or as a graph in selected formats. Strategies such as Open High, Open Low price analyses to comprehend the intraday price changes are also discussed. Through these codes, price trends, investment strategies or equities & options trading can be optimized.

Authors express sincere gratitude to **Mr. K. G. Prakash**, Secretary and College Governing Council of Rajapalayam Rajus' College, Rajapalayam, India for granting consents and for their encouragements to publish our work. Authors are also thankful to **Dr. C. Ramakarishnan**, Principal i/c for his support and motivation to publish this book.

Authors extend their appreciations to Kindle Direct Publishing, Amazon, USA for formatting our work into a book.

**Dr. M Kanagasabapathy**
**Dr. R. Vishnushankar**
**Dr. R. Jaganath**

# About the authors

**Dr. M Kanagasabapathy** is working as Associate Professor, Department of Chemistry, Rajapalayam Rajus' College, affiliated to Madurai Kamaraj University, Rajapalayam, Tamil Nadu, India. He pursued his Ph.D. in Industrial Chemistry at Central Electrochemical Research Institute, Council for Scientific & Industrial Research, Karaikudi, India. He is pursuing electrochemical research works in collaboration with National and International Research Institutes and Universities. He received funds from UGC and MSME, India for electrochemical research works. He has about 31 years of teaching experience in both chemistry as well as chemical engineering disciplines. He received two patents for designing microcontroller modules to test the batteries and supercapatteries, To date, he published 28 research papers, in peer-reviewed, Scopus research journals and designed 24 computer simulation programs coded in Python, MATLAB, Visual Studio and wxMaxima. His computer simulation programs were published in research journals and indexed by renowned software publishers. He published 6 books in the themes, rechargeable batteries, supercapacitors and symbolic computations. He is also serving as the Technical Consultant for Energe Capacitors Pvt. Ltd., Rajapalayam (TN) India to design the EDL supercapacitor electrodes. He is also serving the Coordinator, RRC Incubation center and initiated 6 start-ups.

He published many computer programs, coded in Python & Excel-VBA to fetch and analyze the NSE live option chain data and parameters in Excel for equities and indices (NIFTY and Bank NIFTY) as well as to fetch the historical haircut data for stocks listed in NSE.

**Dr. R. Vishnushankar** is working as Selection Grade Assistant Professor of Commerce in PG Department and Research Centre in Commerce, Rajapalayam Rajus' College, Rajapalayam (Affiliated to Madurai Kamaraj University, Madurai), Tamil Nadu, India. He has a Ph.D. in Commerce from Madurai Kamaraj

University entitled "Performance Evaluation of Indian Mutual Funds – A Comparative Study between the Public Sector and Private Sector Mutual Funds" and he did his Master of Business Administration at Anna University, Chennai. He has 17 Years of teaching experience and 3 Years research experience. He has attended and presented various Seminars, Workshops and Conferences sponsored by UGC, ICSSR, and other funding agencies. He has guided 10 PG students' projects. He published more than 15 peer viewed research paper and ISBN book chapters. He authored Two ISBN book. He administrated various positions in academics; this position includes IQAC Coordinator, Placement Cell - Coordinator, Rajapalayam Rajus' College Alumni Association Treasurer, AISHE – Nodal Officer, UBA 2.0 – Nodal Officer, NIRF – Nodal Officer, RRC – Incubation Centre – Coordinator, NSS Programming Officer and IIC – Executive Member. He organized number of Entrepreneurial Training Programs and Placement drives for college students. He awarded University Level BEST NSS Programme Officer at Madurai Kamaraj University, Madurai, Tamil Nadu.

**Lt. Dr. R. Jaganath**, is working as Associate Professor and Head, PG Department and Research Centre in History, Rajapalayam Rajus' College, Rajapalayam (Affiliated to Madurai Kamaraj University, Madurai), Tamil Nadu, India. He completed Ph.D in History and having 18 Years of teaching experience and 8 Years research experience. He is an Editor for Quest Historia – A Journal of History and Sub Editor for Proceeding of the South Indian History Congress - Journal of History (UGC Care List Journal). He has presented and attended more than 40 research papers in Seminars and Conferences sponsored by UGC, ICHR, ICSSR, Indian History Congress, South Indian History Congress and Tamil Nadu History Congress. He published more than 15 peer viewed research articles, UGC Care list Journal and ISBN book chapters. He has administrative experience in academics as well as extension activities like Coordinator of NSS, NCC, Rotaract Club & Nature Club. He also served as the Principal i/c of

Rajapalayam Rajus' College from 2020 to 2021. He received Madurai Kamaraj University Level Best NSS Programme Officer in 2016, Best Rotaract Coordinator Award by Rotary Club of Rajapalayam in 2018 and also he received National Level Bronze Medal at NCC Officers' Training Academy, Kamptee in 2018.

He has rich experience in Stock Market and has vast experience in Technical Analysis and his expertise lies in extensive use of Price Action based strategies.

**Pre-requisites for the book**

- ✓ Basic knowledge in fundamental as well as technical data analysis of equities & indices.

- ✓ Hands-on experience in Python, Matplotlib coding, and structure of the .csv spreadsheets.

- ✓ Basic knowledge in derivatives market – Futures & Options trading in equities & derivative market.

# Contents

# 1. A brief note about National Stock Exchange

Official website: https://www.nseindia.com/

## 1.1 History & Milestones

The National Stock Exchange (NSE) is a national importance with international stature. It is a trusted market infrastructure organization with rigorous corporate governance requirements in India. The NSE was the first exchange in India to deploy electronic trading, which commenced operations in 1994.

NSE was incorporated in 1992. It was recognised as a stock exchange by SEBI in April 1993 and commenced operations in 1994 with the launch of the wholesale debt market, followed shortly after by the launch of the cash market segment.

| YEAR | MILESTONES |
|---|---|
| 1993 - 1994 | Launched the equity and wholesale debt market segments.<br>Commenced electronic or screen-based trading. |
| 1995 - 1996 | Created and administered a settlement fund<br>Launched NIFTY 50 Index Commenced trading and settlement in dematerialized securities. |

| YEAR | MILESTONES |
|---|---|
| 1997 - 1998 | Established NSE Indices Limited (formerly known as India Index Services & Products Limited) a subsidiary, as a joint venture with CRISIL Limited to operate an indices business. |
| 1998 - 1999 | Established NSEIT, a wholly-owned subsidiary and a global technology firm, that provides end-to-end technology solutions, including application services, infrastructure services, analytics as a service and IT-enabled services. |
| 1999 - 2000 | Incorporated NSE Data & Analytics Limited (formerly known as DotEx International Limited), a wholly-owned subsidiary, and consolidated the data and info-vending business under Data & Analytics Limited. |
| 2000 - 2001 | Launched index options based on the NIFTY 50index (then known as S&PCNX NIFTY) for trading. Launched single stock futures and options on listed securities. |
| 2001 - 2002 | Launched ETF listings. |
| 2004 - 2005 | Launched NIFTY Bank index derivatives. |

| YEAR | MILESTONES |
|---|---|
| 2005 - 2006 | Incorporated NSE InfoTech Ltd., a wholly-owned subsidiary for IT research and development. |
| 2007 - 2008 | Became the first exchange in India to offer trading in Currency Futures.<br>Introduced the Securities Lending and Borrowing Scheme (SLBS).<br>Launched the NOW platform for web-based trading. |
| 2008 - 2009 | Launched Mutual Fund Service System (MFSS). |
| 2009 - 2010 | Launched NOW platform for mobile devices.<br>Launched trading in currency options. |
| 2010 - 2011 | Commenced trading in index futures and options on global indices, namely the S&P 500 and Dow Jones Industrial Average. |
| 2011 - 2012 | Commenced trading in index futures and options contracts on the FTSE 100 index.<br>Launched SME-specific EMERGE platform for the listing and trading of securities of SMEs. |
| 2012 - 2013 | Launched the New Debt Segment (NDS). |

| YEAR | MILESTONES |
|------|------------|
| 2013 - 2014 | Launched NMF-II platform for mutual funds.<br>Launched NBF II segment for interest rate futures.<br>Launched trading on India VIX index futures.<br>Commenced trading on NIFTY 50 (then known as CNX NIFTY) on the Osaka Exchange. |
| 2014 - 2015 | Entered into a memorandum of understanding to enhance co-operation with the London Stock Exchange Group.<br>Renamed CNX NIFTY to NIFTY 50. |
| 2015 - 2016 | Launched NIFTY 50 index futures trading on TAIFEX.<br>Launched platform for sovereign gold bond issuance.<br>Launched an electronic book-building platform for the private placement of debt securities. |
| 2016 - 2017 | Promoted NSE IFSC, the International Stock Exchange in India's first IFSC SEZ at GIFT City Gandhinagar. |
| 2017 - 2018 | Launched currency derivatives on Non-FCYINR pairs<br>Launched NIFTY SME EMERGE Index and 72 fixed income and three hybrid indices.<br>Entered into a MOU with The Colombo Stock Exchange (CSE). |

| YEAR | MILESTONES |
|---|---|
| 2018 - 2019 | Launched Commodity Derivatives segment, go Bid Mobile app for government securities and Tri-Party Repo of Corporate Debt Securities.<br>Weekly option on NIFTY 50 was launched<br>E-voting for corporates.<br>NSE derivatives access was extended to US clients.<br>Signs Post-Trade Technology and Strategic Partnership Agreement with NASDAQ.<br>MoU with London Stock Exchange Group. |
| 2019 - 2020 | NSE launches new brand identity for NIFTY Indices.<br>Proposed NSE IFSC-SGX Connect receives regulatory dispensations.<br>NSE EMERGE achieves 200th SME listing milestone.<br>NSE Commodities Segment gets recognition from CBDT<br>NSE opens Centre for Behavioral Science at IIMA.<br>Launch of Interest Rate Options on Government of India bonds.<br>NSE Indices launches Nifty BHARAT Bond Index Series.<br>NSE declared world's largest derivatives exchange 2019 by WFE.<br>NSE launches Request for Quote (RFQ) Platform in Debt Securities. |
| 2021 - 2022 | NSE launches cloud-based research facility NSE Data Room (NDR).<br>NSE Indices launches Nifty Midcap Select Index.<br>NSE introduces trading of weekly futures on US Dollar - Indian Rupees currency pair. |

| YEAR | MILESTONES |
|---|---|
|  | NSE registered investor base surpasses 5 crore unique investors.<br>NSE Indices launches Nifty India Digital Index.<br>India celebrates Silver Jubilee of NIFTY 50 Index and 20 Years of Derivatives in Indian Capital Market.<br>NSE Indices launches Nifty Transportation & Logistics Index.<br>NSE IFSC becomes First International Exchange at IFSC to physically settle US Stocks.<br>NSE Indices launches Nifty SDL Plus AAA PSU Bond Dec 2027 60:40 Index.<br>NSE Indices launches Nifty SDL Jun 2027 Index.<br>NSE and IBJA to come together to set-up Domestic Bullion Spot Exchange.<br>NSE Data launches Fixed Income Analytics Platform (FixedIn).<br>NSE IFSC-SGX Connect Inaugurated. |
| 2022 - 2023 | World's Largest Derivative Exchange in terms of contracts traded.<br>22 years of partnership between NSE and SGX for NIFTY50. |
| 2023 - 2024 | World's Largest Derivative Exchange in terms of contracts traded.<br>Unveiling of NSE IX and Gift Nifty Logo at Gift City<br>Launch of Gift Nifty Trading at NSE IX, Gifty City<br>First listing on NSE Social Stock Exchange.<br>Nifty50 touches 20000 on Sept 11, 2023, 21000 on Dec 8, 2023 and 25000 on Aug 1, 2024. |

## 1.2 Records of NSE

Some of the highest records of NSE for indices and capital market are listed to highlight the volume of trades and turnover.

### Indices

| # | Index | Highest Intra-Day value |
|---|---|---|
| 1 | Nifty 50 | 26,277.35  (Sep 27, 2024) |
| 2 | Nifty Bank | 54,467.35 (Sep 26, 2024) |
| 3 | Nifty Financial Services | 25,201.95 (Sep 26, 2024) |
| 4 | Nifty Midcap Select | 13,407.55 (Sep 16, 2024) |
| 5 | Nifty Next 50 | 77,918.00 (Sep 27, 2024) |

### Capital Market

| # | Particulars | Date | Value |
|---|---|---|---|
| 1 | Number of trades | Jun 04, 2024 | 88,505,365 |
| 2 | Turnover (INR, Cr.) | Jun 04, 2024 | 2,71,245.43 |
| 3 | Market Cap. (INR, Cr.) | Sep 27, 2024 | 4,73,83,695.36 |
| 4 | Total traded quantity (Number of shares in lakhs) | Apr 25, 2024 | 1,18,127.43 |

## Equity Derivatives

| # | Particulars | Date | Value |
|---|---|---|---|
| 1 | Number of trades | Jun 19, 2024 | 24,25,13,525 |
| 2 | Total traded contracts | Feb 14, 2024 | 1,03,51,46,752 |
| 3 | Total traded value (INR, Cr.) | Jun 04, 2024 | 7,04,024.06 |

## Instrument wise turnover

| # | Particulars | Date | Value (INR, Cr.) |
|---|---|---|---|
| 1 | Index Futures | Jun 04, 2024 | 1,57,036.06 |
| 2 | Index Options (Premium) | Jun 04, 2024 | 2,13,406.13 |
| 3 | Stock Futures | Jul 23, 2024 | 3,98,160.77 |
| 4 | Stock Options (Premium) | Jun 04, 2024 | 20,682.59 |

## Currency Derivatives

| Sr No. | Particulars | Date | Value |
|---|---|---|---|
| 1 | Number of trades | Nov 11, 2022 | 11,40,451 |
| 2 | Total traded contracts | Mar 22, 2024 | 47,934,369 |
| 3 | Total traded value (INR, Cr.) | Mar 22, 2024 | 99,910.80 |

## 2. Basics of derivatives market

A derivative market is a financial market where derivative instruments are traded. Derivatives are financial securities that derive their value from an underlying asset, such as:

Stocks (equities)

Commodities (gold, oil, etc.)

Currencies (forex)

Indices (Nifty, Sensex, etc.)

Interest rates

### 2.1 Types of Derivatives:

<u>Futures</u>

A Futures contract is an agreement to buy or sell an underlying asset at a predetermined price on a specific date.

<u>Options</u>

An Options contract gives the buyer the right, but not the obligation, to buy or sell an underlying asset at a predetermined price on or before a specific date.

Futures & Options (FnO) are used for trading and used for hedging. Options are more popular and has many strike prices unlike Futures and has many options to hedge.

Index Options such as Bank NIFTY, NIFTY has weekly expiry where as Stock options has monthly expiry.

## 2.2 Important keywords in options trading

Option Chain

An option chain is a table that displays all available options contracts for a particular underlying asset. It consists of

Calls (CE) and Puts (PE)

Strike Prices

Expiration Dates

Bid and Ask Prices

Open Interest and Volume

CE (Call Option, European)

A call option gives the buyer the right to buy the underlying asset at the strike price.

PE (Put Option, European)

A put option gives the buyer the right to sell the underlying asset at the strike price.

Strike Price

Predetermined price at which the option can be exercised.

Underlying Price

Current market price of the underlying asset, Index or equity. Based on this the premium for CE and PE for strike prices changes.

Intrinsic Value

Difference between the strike price and the current market price or the underlying price.

## Options Premium

Options premium is the price paid by the buyer to the seller for an options contract. It's an important component of options trading. Its value depends on time and in the money or out of the money of the strike price.

## Call Premium

Premium paid for a call option at the selected strike price.

## Put Premium

Premium paid for a put option at the selected strike price.

## Volatility Value (or) Implied Volatility

Change in the price of an equity or index with time is termed as volatility. If the change is high, then volatility is higher and the price of an equity or index moves swiftly up and down. Volatility is low, if the rate of price of an equity or index is low. IV indicates the expected volatility of the underlying asset.

## Time to Expiration

The remaining time until expiration.

## Time Value

The value of the option's remaining time until expiration.

## Liquidity Risk:

Difficulty exiting positions. For example, on expiry day if the strike price comes in the money (ITM) for a stock option.

## For Call Option

In-the-Money (ITM): Underlying price > Strike price

Buy call option at strike price 100, underlying price 110

Intrinsic value = 110 - 100 = 10

Out-of-the-Money (OTM): Underlying price < Strike price

Sell call option at strike price 110, underlying price 100.

No intrinsic value

At-the-Money (ATM): Underlying price = Strike price

Buy call option at strike price 100, underlying price 100.

No intrinsic value

<u>For Put Option</u>

In-the-Money (ITM): Underlying price < Strike price

Buy put option at strike price 100, underlying price 90

Intrinsic value = 100 - 90 = 10

Out-of-the-Money (OTM): Underlying price > Strike price

Sell put option with strike price 90, underlying price 100

No intrinsic value

At-the-Money (ATM): Underlying price = Strike price

Buy put option with strike price 100, underlying price 100

No intrinsic value

<u>Option Greeks</u>

Option Greeks (OG) are measures used to assess the risk and potential profit of options trading. They quantify the sensitivity of options prices to changes in underlying factors. Some of the basic OG are briefed out:

<u>Delta (Δ)</u>

Measures the rate of change of the option's price with respect to the underlying asset's price.

Call option delta: 0.5 to 1

Put option delta: -1 to -0.5

Gamma (Γ)

Measures the rate of change of delta with respect to the underlying asset's price.

High gamma: Delta changes rapidly

Low gamma: Delta changes slowly

Vega (v)

Measures the rate of change of the option's price with respect to volatility.

High vega: Option price sensitive to volatility changes.

Low vega: Option price less sensitive to volatility.

Theta (θ)

Measures the rate of change of the option's price with respect to time.

High theta: Option price decreases rapidly with time.

Low theta: Option price decreases slowly with time.

Rho (ρ)

Measures the rate of change of the option's price with respect to interest rates.

High rho: Option price sensitive to interest rate changes.

Low rho: Option price less sensitive.

Epsilon (ε)

Measures the rate of change of the option's price with respect to underlying asset's price volatility.

Importance of Option Greeks:

Lambda (λ)

Measures the rate of change of the option's price with respect to dividend yield.

OG can be useful for option traders with reference to risk management, to identify the volatility, to observe the time decay of premium and to hedge the positions.

Following Image illustrates the ATM, ITM, OTM and Intrinsic values of the option chain for CE and PE values.

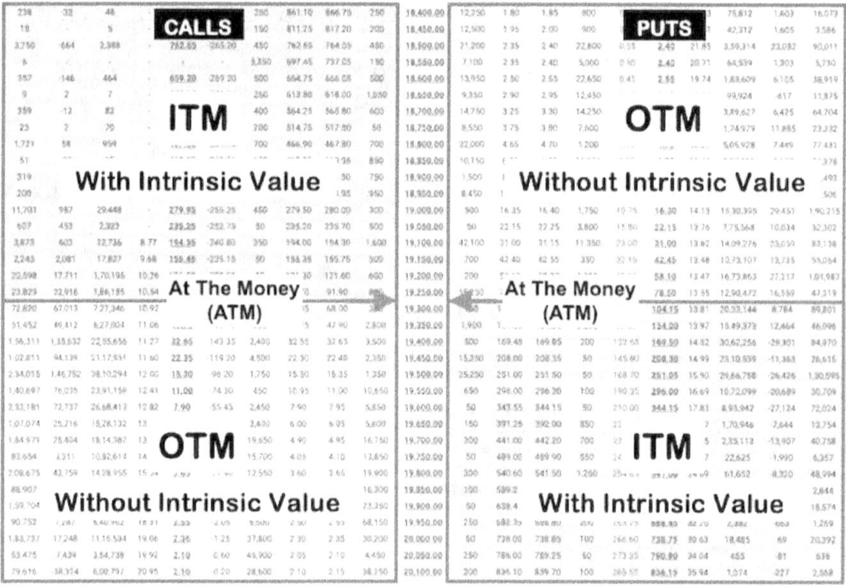

## 3. Why Python for stock market data?

Python is a preferred language for stock market data analysis for several reasons. Derivatives, Index and individual equity data are numerical and Python is a powerful tool and can be deployed for numerical data analyzes and also has the capability in web scrapping to fetch the historical data. Some of the key strengths of Python, which is specific for this domain are:

### 3.1. Rich libraries and frameworks

Python offers a wide range of libraries like Pandas, NumPy, Matplotlib, SciPy, and Stats models. These libraries simplify data manipulation, statistical analysis, and visualization, which are essential for stock market data analysis.

### 3.2. Data handling capabilities

numpy and pandas allows for fast and efficient data handling, such as filtering, sorting, and aggregating time-series data like stock prices. It also makes it easy to work with large datasets, which is common in the financial markets. The fetched data can be analyzed and can be saved as Excel or .csv file.

### 3.3. Easy integration with APIs

Python can easily integrate with stock market data APIs like Yahoo Finance, Alpha Vantage, and NSE, allowing real-time and historical data fetching. This capability simplifies the automation of data collection processes. There are several Python tools and libraries that can be used to integrate with the NSE India APIs to fetch live stock market data.

### 3.4. Visualization tools

Libraries like Matplotlib, Seaborn, and Plotly offer powerful tools for data visualization, making it easier to plot stock prices, trends, and technical indicators.

### 3.5. Machine Learning and AI integration

Python excels in the integration of machine learning models for predictive analysis using libraries such as Scikit-learn, TensorFlow, and Keras. This makes it easy to develop and deploy predictive models for stock price forecasting and algorithmic trading.

### 3.6. Community and open-source

Python has a massive community, and the open-source nature of its ecosystem allows access to pre-built financial models, libraries, and frameworks that simplify stock market analysis.

### 3.7. Fast prototyping

Python's simple syntax and readability make it easier to write quick scripts, allowing analysts to experiment with models and strategies faster compared to other languages like Java or C++.

### 3.8. Back-testing libraries

Python supports dedicated back-testing libraries like Backtrader and PyAlgoTrade. These libraries allow traders to test their strategies on historical data to assess performance before applying them in live markets.

### 3.9. Time series analysis

Python libraries like Statsmodels and PyFlux offer built-in support for time series analysis, enabling robust analysis of stock prices, which are inherently time-dependent.

### 3.10. Web scraping tools

Python's libraries like BeautifulSoup and Selenium are excellent for scraping stock market data from websites, enabling users to gather data from multiple sources when API access is restricted.

### 3.11. Open source and scalable

Since Python is open-source and scalable, it offers a cost-effective way to analyze large amounts of stock market data, making it ideal for both individual traders, investors and even for large firms.

### 3.12. Cross-platform compatibility

Python can run on different platforms (Windows, MacOS, Linux operating systems), making it easy to develop stock market analysis tools that work across various operating systems.

These strengths collectively make Python a go-to language for stock market data analysis. Its versatility, simplicity, and powerful libraries enable efficient data manipulation, model building, and strategy testing in financial markets.

## 4. How to fetch JSON file from NSE website?

JSON (JavaScript Object Notation) file is a text-based format for storing and exchanging data and can be readable by humans as well as computers. And it is light-weight and widely used to store larger data. In NSE website, market data for equities as well as derivatives (futures & options) are stored as NSE.

To fetch the market data information, relevant JSON file should be identified. Following step by step illustrations show, how to identify the JSON file for the selected stock. This illustration is based on the equity, SBIN (State Bank of India).

### 4.1 Getting the JSON live link

<u>Step 1</u>

Go to NSE India website: https://www.nseindia.com/ And search for the equity by its symbol (example: SBIN).

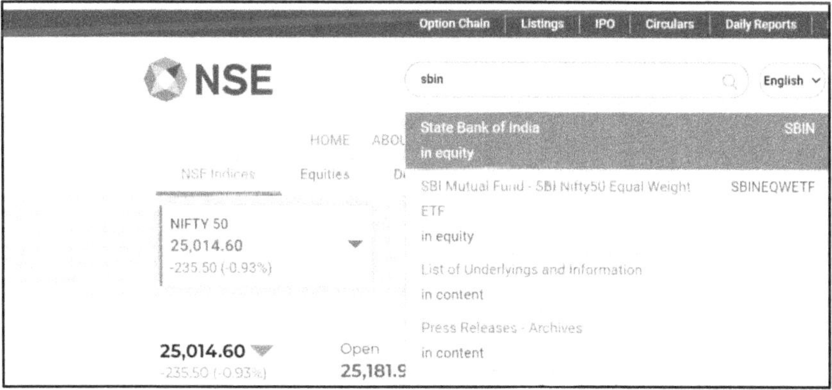


Check for the traded data. This gives the trades and price information such as Last Traded Price, Open, Previous Close

Price, Low, High etc., for the selected equity on that time. In live market hours, these values will be updated periodically.

## Step 2

Then right click the page and select 'Inspect' to access the data source.

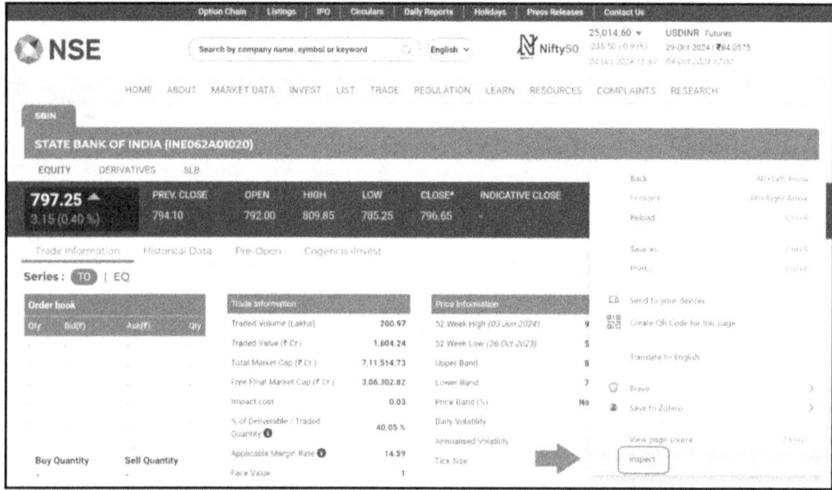

## Step 3

Ensure 'Equity' tab is selected. Then click 'Network' and ensure tab is selected at Fetch/XHR.

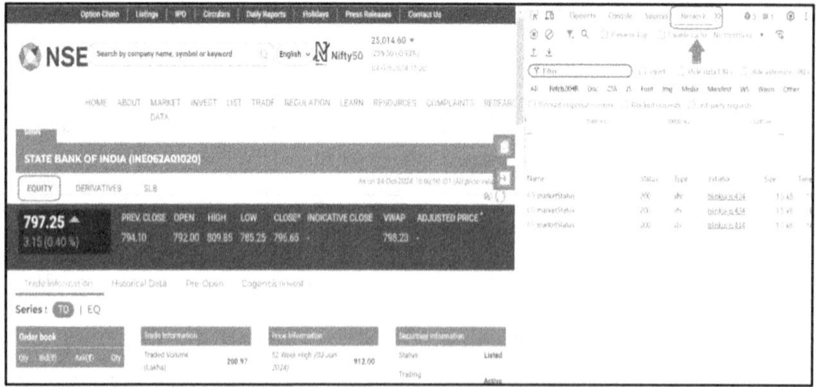

<u>Step 4</u>

Then Refresh the page. (CTRL+R for Windows). This leads to load many files and click each file individaully and identify the correct JSON file with required data.

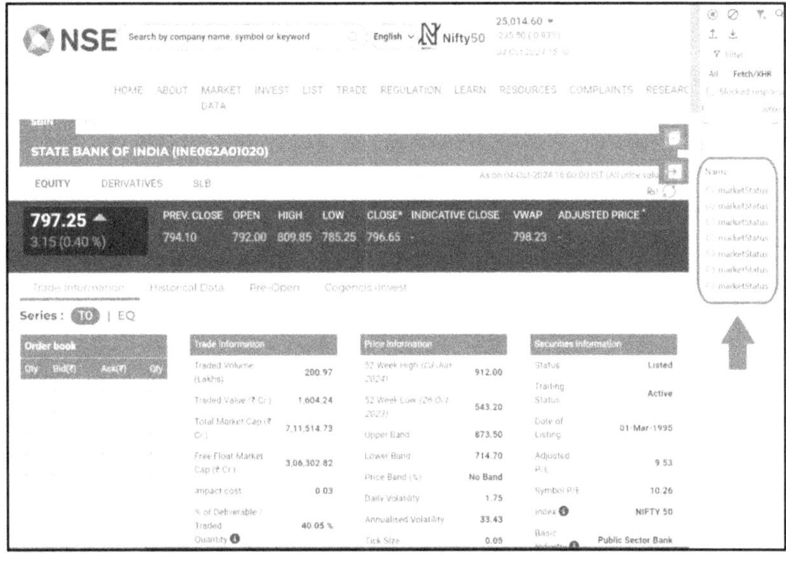

On refresh, loads many data files.

Identify the required JSON file.

## 4.2 JSON beautification

Since the data is unreadable and clumsy, use the Pretty-print option from the web browser or online JSON beautifier (to make it readable) with the JSON hyperlink from NSE website. If necessary, use free online JSON beautifier tools to read the data from the JSON file. Some browsers have built-in capabilities for JSON file beautification such as Pretty-print in Brave web browser. This makes the JSON file readable.

For SBIN, the identified JSON link for equity price and trade data is:  https://www.nseindia.com/api/quote-equity?symbol=SBIN

 For RELIANCE industries the JSON link file is:

https://www.nseindia.com/api/quote-equity?symbol=RELIANCE

For Tata Consultancy Services (TCS) the JSON link file is:

https://www.nseindia.com/api/quote-equity?symbol=TCS


Note that the last part is replaced with the equity symbol. JSON link shows the data like this.

Pretty-print

{"info":{"symbol":"SBIN","companyName":"State Bank of India","industry":"Public Sector Bank","activeSeries":["EQ","T0"],"debtSeries":[],"isFNOSec":true,"isCASec":false,"isSLBSec":true,"isDebtSec":false,"isSuspended":false,"tempSuspendedSeries":["N3","N6","N5","IL","N1","N2","N4"],"isETFSec":false,"isDelisted":false,"isin":"INE062A08041","slb_isin":"INE062A01020","isMunicipalBond":false,"isTop10":false,"identifier":"{"series":"EQ","symbol":"SBIN","isin":"INE062A01020","status":"Listed","listingDate":"01-Mar-1995","industry":"Public Sector Bank","lastUpdateTime":"04-Oct-2024 16:00:00","pdSectorPe":9.53,"pdSymbolPe":10.26,"pdSectorInd":"NIFTY 50","pdSectorIndAll":["NIFTY 50","NIFTY BANK","NIFTY FINANCIAL SERVICES","NIFTY 200","NIFTY 500","NIFTY50 15","NIFTY DIVIDEND OPPORTUNITIES 50","NIFTY HIGH BETA 50","NIFTY HOUSING","NIFTY500 VALUE 50","NIFTY ALPHA LOW-VOLATILITY 30","NIFTY50 EQUAL WEIGHT","NIFTY FINANCIAL SERVICE 250","NIFTY RURAL","NIFTY200 VALUE 30","NIFTY500 EQUAL WEIGHT","NIFTY100 ESG","NIFTY TOTAL MARKET","NIFTY500 MULTICAP 50:25:25","NIFTY500 LARGEMIDSMALL EQUAL-CAP WEIGHTED","N BANK","NIFTY 100","NIFTY100 EQUAL WEIGHT"]},"securityInfo":{"boardStatus":"Main","tradingStatus":"Active","tradingSegment":"Normal Market","sessionNo":"-","slb":"Yes","classOfShare":"Equity","derivatives":"Yes","surveillance":{"surv":null,"desc":null},"faceValue":1,"issuedSize":8924612434},"sddDetails":{"SDDAuditor":"-","SDDS{"lastPrice":797.25,"change":3.14999999999998,"pChange":0.396675481677368,"previousClose":794.1,"open":792,"close":796.65,"vwap":798.23,"stockIndClosePrice":null,"lowerCP":"7 nd":"No Band","basePrice":794.1,"intraDayHighLow":{"min":785.25,"max":809.85,"value":797.25},"weekHighLow":{"min":543.2,"minDate":"26-Oct-2023","max":912,"maxDate":"03-Jun-2024","value":797.25},"iNavValue":null,"checkINAV":false,"tickSize":0.05},"industryInfo":{"macro":"Financial Services","sector":"Financial Services","industry":"Banks","basic Bank"},"preOpenMarket":{"preopen":[{"price":724.1,"buyQty":0,"sellQty":100},{"price":750,"buyQty":0,"sellQty":30},{"price":751,"buyQty":0,"sellQty":1000},{"price":754,"buyQty {"price":792,"buyQty":0,"sellQty":0,"iep":true},{"price":829.8,"buyQty":131,"sellQty":0},{"price":830.1,"buyQty":2,"sellQty":0},{"price":833.8,"buyQty":2,"sellQty":0},{"price":836.75,"buyQty":4,"sellQty":0}],"ato":{"buy":3660,"sell":2808},"IEP":792,"totalTradedVolume":25743,"finalPrice":792,"finalQuantity":25743,"lastUpdateTime":"04-Oct-20 09:07:44","totalBuyQuantity":90079,"totalSellQuantity":217884,"atoBuyQty":3660,"atoSellQty":2808,"Change":-2.10000000000002,"perChange":-0.26445032111825,"prevClose":794.1}}

JSON data with Pretty-print option of the web browser (Brave).

```
Pretty-print ☑
    },
    "priceInfo": {
      "lastPrice": 797.25,
      "change": 3.14999999999998,
      "pChange": 0.396675481677368,
      "previousClose": 794.1,
      "open": 792,
      "close": 796.65,
      "vwap": 798.23,
      "stockIndClosePrice": null,
      "lowerCP": "714.70",
      "upperCP": "873.50",
      "pPriceBand": "No Band",
      "basePrice": 794.1,
      "intraDayHighLow": {
        "min": 785.25,
        "max": 809.85,
        "value": 797.25
      },
      "weekHighLow": {
        "min": 543.2,
        "minDate": "26-Oct-2023",
        "max": 912,
        "maxDate": "03-Jun-2024",
        "value": 797.25
      },
```

Sometimes the JSON URL may show error with online JSON beautifiers. In such case, to beautify the JSON data to readable format, the data can also be saved (by right clicking in the web page and selecting the save as option) as .json file and can be uploaded in JSON beautifier.

By inferring this, the keywords against the required data should be noted and can be deployed in the Python code to fetch or to analyze the data.

JSON file after the beautification with online JSON beautifier.

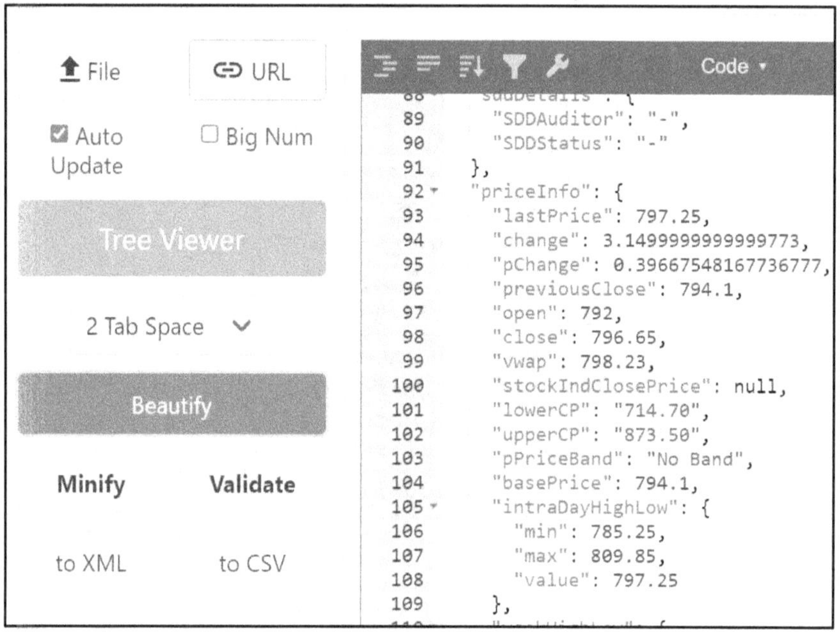


It must be emphasized that the JSON link shows error on sometimes and no data will be fetched. It depends on the NSE server, blocking the IP address, latency etc.

The JSON file from the NSE India website either for equities or for Index is rich of data and from the keywords, or key values corresponding to the required data, numerical values can be fetched through Python coding.

JSON file will be updated at specific intervals, in live market hours and real-time data can be fetched.

Screenshot of the JSON data for Infosys from NIFTY 100 Index.

```json
{
  "priority": 0,
  "symbol": "INFY",
  "identifier": "INFYEQN",
  "series": "EQ",
  "open": 1918,
  "dayHigh": 1926.7,
  "dayLow": 1910.1,
  "lastPrice": 1921.75,
  "previousClose": 1919,
  "change": 2.75,
  "pChange": 0.14,
  "totalTradedVolume": 192498,
  "stockIndClosePrice": 0,
  "totalTradedValue": 369032140.86,
  "lastUpdateTime": "11-Oct-2024 09:15:44",
  "yearHigh": 1977,
  "ffmc": 6891727812873.84,
  "yearLow": 1351.65,
  "nearWKH": 2.79463834092059,
  "nearWKL": -42.1780786446195,
  "perChange365d": 28.41,
  "date365dAgo": "11-Oct-2023",
  "chart365dPath": "https://nsearchives.nseindia.com/365d/INFY-EQ.svg",
  "date30dAgo": "10-Sep-2024",
  "perChange30d": 0.35,
  "chart30dPath": "https://nsearchives.nseindia.com/30d/INFY-EQ.svg",
  "chartTodayPath": "https://nsearchives.nseindia.com/today/INFYEQN.svg",
```

The keywords are mostly self-explanatory.

Example: "ffmc" stands for Free Float Market Cap.

"perChange365d" refers the Percentage change in 1 year.

By identifying the specific keywords, required data can be fetched and it must be emphasized that these data in JSON link will be updated periodically at specific intervals during live market hours. It is prudent to this JSON data can be downloaded and saved in local directory for further analysis rather than fetching with the live link. Because NSE restricts or block the IP for the multiple access of JSON by refreshing the link in browser.

# 5. JSON file structure

A JSON (JavaScript Object Notation) file represents data in a structured format using key-value pairs. It is primarily used for storing and transmitting large data between a server and a web client due to its lightweight and readability.

## 5.1 Basic elements of JSON:

### a. Objects:

These are enclosed in {} (curly braces) and consist of key-value pairs. The keys are strings (in double quotes), and values can be of different data types (e.g., string, number, array, object, boolean, or null).

Example:

```
{
  "name": "Santhosh",
  "age": 41,
  "isEmployed": true
}
```

In this object:

"name" is a key with the value "John" (a string).

"age" is a key with the value 30 (a number).

"isEmployed" is a key with the value true (a boolean).

### b. Arrays:

These are enclosed in [] (square brackets) and can contain multiple values, which can be objects, strings, numbers, etc.

Example:

```
{
  "employees": [
    { "name": "Santhosh", "age": 41 },
    { "name": "Pooja", "age": 35 }
  ]
}
```

In this structure:

"employees" is a key with an array as its value.

The array contains two objects, each representing an employee.

## 5.2 JSON file structure:

The structure of a JSON file is nested with objects and arrays, which can contain further objects and arrays, creating a hierarchy of data.

Example:

```
{
  "company": "Stock anlaysts",
  "location": "Mumbai",
  "departments": [
    {
      "name": "Development",
      "employees": [
        { "name": "Santhosh", "role": "Developer"
},
        { "name": "Pooja", "role": "Tester" }
      ]
    },
    {
      "name": "HR",
      "employees": [
        { "name": "John", "role": "Recruiter" }
      ]
    }
```

```
    ],
    "isHiring": true,
    "established": 1999
  }
```

In this structure:

The root object has keys like "company", "location", "departments", "isHiring", and "established".

"departments" is an array containing two objects, each representing a department.

Each department object contains a "name" and an "employees" key, where "employees" is an array containing employee objects.

## 5.3 Structure specific to JSON data from APIs:

For example, if we consider a JSON response from a stock market API (like those provided by NSE India), the structure follows a nested format:

```
{
  "info": {
    "symbol": "SBIN",
    "lastUpdateTime": "2024-10-07T14:30:00+05:30",
    "priceInfo": {
      "lastPrice": 512.45,
      "change": 4.5,
      "pChange": 0.88
    },
    "marketState": "OPEN"
  },
  "metadata": {
    "exchange": "NSE",
    "sector": "Banking"
  }
}
```

Here, the root object contains:

"info": an object containing keys like "symbol",

"lastUpdateTime", and "priceInfo".

"priceInfo" itself is an object with keys like "lastPrice",

"change", and "pChange".

"metadata": another object containing information about

the exchange and sector.

## 5.4 Structural components for JSON url from NSE

For the equity the JSON url, related to the trade information from the NSE website is:

https://www.nseindia.com/api/quote-equity?symbol=SBIN

And the snippet of the beautified output is:

```
{
  "info": {
    "symbol": "SBIN",
    "lastUpdateTime": "2024-10-07T14:30:00+05:30",
    "priceInfo": {
      "lastPrice": 512.45,
      "change": 4.5,
      "pChange": 0.88,
      "open": 508.00,
      "dayHigh": 514.50,
      "dayLow": 507.00,
      "close": 507.95
    }
  },
  "marketDeptOrderBook": {
    "totalBuyQuantity": 200000,
    "totalSellQuantity": 150000,
    "bid": [
      { "price": 511.00, "quantity": 5000 },
      { "price": 510.00, "quantity": 3000 }
    ],
    "ask": [
      { "price": 513.00, "quantity": 4000 },
      { "price": 514.00, "quantity": 2500 }
```

```
    ]
  },
  "securityInfo": {
    "isin": "INE062A01020",
    "industry": "Banking",
    "tradingSymbol": "SBIN"
  },
  "metadata": {
    "exchange": "NSE",
    "series": "EQ"
  }
}
```

## 5.5 Breakdown of structural components:

The JSON file contains several nested objects, each holding specific data related to the stock.

Some of the key components are:

info: Contains general information about the stock.

symbol: The stock symbol (e.g., "SBIN").

lastUpdateTime: Timestamp of the last update for the stock data.

priceInfo: An object with detailed pricing information.

priceInfo: Contains information about the stock's price and changes.

lastPrice: The latest trading price of the stock.

change: The absolute change in the price since the previous trading session.

pChange: The percentage change in the price.

open: The price at which the stock opened in the current session.

dayHigh: The highest price of the stock during the trading session.

dayLow: The lowest price of the stock during the trading session.

close: The closing price from the previous trading session.

marketDeptOrderBook: Contains details about the order book, showing buy and sell quantities.

totalBuyQuantity: The total quantity available for purchase.

totalSellQuantity: The total quantity available for selling.

bid and ask: Arrays containing information about different bid and ask prices and quantities.

securityInfo: Information about the stock's classification and market status.

isin: International Securities Identification Number.

industry: Industry sector to which the stock belongs.

tradingSymbol: The symbol used for trading.

metadata: Includes details about the stock's trading status.

exchange: Indicates the exchange where the stock is listed.

series: Represents the type of stock (e.g., EQ for equity).

In concise:

'info' provides the basic identification and price details.

'priceInfo' is gives the price movements and daily statistics.

'marketDeptOrderBook' gives the buy/sell demand and liquidity.

'securityInfo' and 'metadata' give additional context about the market listing and industry classification.

# 6. Trade and price data for equity

For investors and traders, the most important info required is the last traded price (LTP) and the change in the price. Following code exemplifies the collection of the data from the JSON link for SBIN.

**<u>Code</u>**

```python
import requests
# Define the URL for the JSON data
url         =         "https://www.nseindia.com/api/quote-equity?symbol=SBIN"

# Define headers (NSE website may require these headers)
headers = {
    'User-Agent': 'Mozilla/5.0 (Windows NT 10.0; Win64; x64) AppleWebKit/537.36 (KHTML, like Gecko) Chrome/58.0.3029.110 Safari/537.3',
    'Accept-Language': 'en-US,en;q=0.9',
    'Accept-Encoding': 'gzip, deflate, br',
    'Connection': 'keep-alive'
}

# Function to fetch and extract the required data
def fetch_price_info():
    try:
        # Start a session to handle cookies
        session = requests.Session()

        # Get the homepage to establish session cookies
        session.get("https://www.nseindia.com",
headers=headers)

        # Send the actual GET request to the data URL
        response = session.get(url, headers=headers)
        response.raise_for_status()  # Raise an exception
for HTTP errors

        # Parse the JSON response
        data = response.json()

        # Extract symbol from "info"
```

```python
        symbol = data['info'].get('symbol')
        # Extract data from "priceInfo"
        price_info = data['priceInfo']
        intra_day_high_low = price_info['intraDayHighLow']

        # Create a dictionary with the required fields
        extracted_data = {
            "Symbol": symbol,
            "LTP": price_info.get('lastPrice'),
            "Price                             change":
round(price_info.get('change'),4),
            "Price            change            (%)":
round(price_info.get('pChange'),4),
            "Previous                            Close":
price_info.get('previousClose'),
            "Open": price_info.get('open'),
            "Close": price_info.get('close'),
            "VWAP": price_info.get('vwap'),
            "Low": intra_day_high_low.get('min'),
            "High": intra_day_high_low.get('max'),
            "Value": intra_day_high_low.get('value')
        }

        # Print the extracted data
        for key, value in extracted_data.items():
            print(f"{key}: {value}")

    except requests.exceptions.RequestException as e:
        print(f"Error occurred: {e}")

# Run the module to fetch and print the price info data
fetch_price_info()
```

**<u>Output</u>**
```
Symbol: SBIN
LTP: 797.25
Price change: 3.15
Price change (%): 0.3967
Previous Close: 794.1
Open: 792
Close: 796.65
VWAP: 798.23
Low: 785.25
High: 809.85
Value: 797.25
```

## 7. Extracting historical price data

Though it is possible to get the .csv file for the historical price for the given equity, in order to analyze and to compare the price trend, following code is used based on the equity ITC. JSON link for the last one month (07-Sep-2024 to 07-Oct-2024) is:

https://www.nseindia.com/api/historical/cm/equity?symbol=ITC

Beautified snippet of the JSON file is:

```
{
  "data": [
    {
      "_id": "6703cd7fdf426bdeedb4e13b",
      "CH_SYMBOL": "ITC",
      "CH_SERIES": "EQ",
      "CH_MARKET_TYPE": "N",
      "CH_TIMESTAMP": "2024-10-07",
      "TIMESTAMP": "2024-10-06T18:30:00.000Z",
      "CH_TRADE_HIGH_PRICE": 514.95,
      "CH_TRADE_LOW_PRICE": 506.75,
      "CH_OPENING_PRICE": 507,
      "CH_CLOSING_PRICE": 510.2,
      "CH_LAST_TRADED_PRICE": 510,
      "CH_PREVIOUS_CLS_PRICE": 503.55,
      "CH_TOT_TRADED_QTY": 16479772,
      "CH_TOT_TRADED_VAL": 8421688874.45,
      "CH_52WEEK_HIGH_PRICE": 528.5,
      "CH_52WEEK_LOW_PRICE": 399.35,
      "CH_TOTAL_TRADES": 216682,
      "CH_ISIN": "INE154A01025",
      "createdAt": "2024-10-07T12:01:03.235Z",
      "updatedAt": "2024-10-07T12:01:03.235Z",
      "__v": 0,
      "SLBMH_TOT_VAL": null,
      "VWAP": 511.03,
      "mTIMESTAMP": "07-Oct-2024"
    },
```

Following code fetches the date, closing price and the VWAP values from the relevant keys.

## Code

```python
import requests
import time

# Define the URL
url = "https://www.nseindia.com/api/historical/cm/equity?symbol=ITC"

# Define headers to mimic a browser
headers = {
    "User-Agent": "Mozilla/5.0 (Windows NT 10.0; Win64; x64) AppleWebKit/537.36 (KHTML, like Gecko) Chrome/58.0.3029.110 Safari/537.3",
    "Accept-Language": "en-US,en;q=0.9",
    "Accept-Encoding": "gzip, deflate, br",
    "Referer": "https://www.nseindia.com",
    "Connection": "keep-alive",
    "DNT": "1",
}

# Function to fetch data with a session to maintain cookies
def fetch_data_with_session(url, headers):
    session = requests.Session()
    session.headers.update(headers)

    # Visit the NSE home page first to establish cookies
    try:
        session.get("https://www.nseindia.com", timeout=10)
        time.sleep(2)  # Wait to avoid being blocked

        # Now request the actual data
        response = session.get(url, timeout=10)
        response.raise_for_status()  # Raise an error for bad responses
        return response.json()
    except requests.exceptions.HTTPError as errh:
        print("HTTP Error:", errh)
    except requests.exceptions.ConnectionError as errc:
        print("Error Connecting:", errc)
    except requests.exceptions.Timeout as errt:
        print("Timeout Error:", errt)
    except requests.exceptions.RequestException as err:
        print("Something went wrong:", err)
```

```python
# Fetch the JSON data
data = fetch_data_with_session(url, headers)

# Extract and display data if available
if data:
    # Extract 'CH_TIMESTAMP', 'CH_CLOSING_PRICE', and
'VWAP' from the 'data' section
    records = data.get('data', [])
    if records:
        # Print the headers
        print(f"{'Date':<20}       {'Close      Price':<20}
{'VWAP':<20}")
        print("-" * 60)

        # Loop through the records and print each row
        for record in records:
            ch_timestamp    =    record.get("CH_TIMESTAMP",
"N/A")
            ch_closing_price                              =
record.get("CH_CLOSING_PRICE", "N/A")
            vwap = record.get("VWAP", "N/A")
            print(f"{ch_timestamp:<20}
{ch_closing_price:<20} {vwap:<20}")
    else:
        print("No records available.")
else:
    print("No data available or failed to fetch data.")
```

**<u>Output</u>**

```
Date                  Close Price          VWAP
------------------------------------------------------------
2024-10-07            510.2                511.03
2024-10-04            503.55               509.93
2024-10-03            512.75               512.47
2024-10-01            516.2                515.9
2024-09-30            518.15               518.56
2024-09-27            522.7                524.14
2024-09-26            522.75               521.19
2024-09-25            517.55               515.67
2024-09-24            515.25               515.47
2024-09-23            516.95               516.88
2024-09-20            514.4                513.97
2024-09-19            508.25               510.59
```

| | | |
|---|---|---|
| 2024-09-18 | 507.35 | 509.15 |
| 2024-09-17 | 507.75 | 508.55 |
| 2024-09-16 | 511.1 | 513.15 |
| 2024-09-13 | 513.85 | 513.81 |
| 2024-09-12 | 519.5 | 515.6 |
| 2024-09-11 | 514.35 | 516.48 |
| 2024-09-10 | 513.6 | 512.86 |
| 2024-09-09 | 511.75 | 509.47 |

<u>Possible known error with this code:</u>

Output as:

```
HTTP Error: 401 Client Error: Unauthorized for url:
https://www.nseindia.com/api/historical/cm/equity?symbol=
ITCNo data available or failed to fetch data.
```

The 401 Unauthorized error indicates that the server requires authentication or that there are restrictions on accessing the API. For the NSE India website, such errors are often due to:

Missing or Incorrect Headers: The NSE India website often checks for headers like User-Agent and Referer to verify that the request comes from a valid browser session.

Session Management: The NSE API might require a session cookie that is typically obtained by visiting the website manually before making an API request programmatically.

Access Restrictions: The API may be restricted to specific IP addresses or regions.

To address these issues, few adjustments can be done:

Add More Headers: Use headers that mimic a real browser request, including cookies if necessary.

Establish a Session: Use requests.Session() to maintain cookies and session information across requests.

Include a Delay: Avoid making frequent requests that may trigger security measures.

## 8. Visualizing historical data: Plotting a graph

To get a graphical interface, plot between Date and Prices can be done. It visualizes the price trend with time. Following code gives the graphical output, instead of numerical data with Date vs Price and this requires matplotlib.

**Code**
```python
import requests
import time
import matplotlib.pyplot as plt

# Define the URL
url = "https://www.nseindia.com/api/historical/cm/equity?symbol=ITC"

# Define headers to mimic a browser
headers = {
    "User-Agent": "Mozilla/5.0 (Windows NT 10.0; Win64; x64) AppleWebKit/537.36 (KHTML, like Gecko) Chrome/58.0.3029.110 Safari/537.3",
    "Accept-Language": "en-US,en;q=0.9",
    "Accept-Encoding": "gzip, deflate, br",
    "Referer": "https://www.nseindia.com",
    "Connection": "keep-alive",
    "DNT": "1",
}

# Function to fetch data with a session to maintain cookies
def fetch_data_with_session(url, headers):
    session = requests.Session()
    session.headers.update(headers)

    # Visit the NSE home page first to establish cookies
    try:
        session.get("https://www.nseindia.com", timeout=10)
        time.sleep(2)  # Wait to avoid being blocked

        # Now request the actual data
```

```python
        response = session.get(url, timeout=10)
        response.raise_for_status()  # Raise an error for
bad responses
        return response.json()
    except requests.exceptions.HTTPError as errh:
        print("HTTP Error:", errh)
    except requests.exceptions.ConnectionError as errc:
        print("Error Connecting:", errc)
    except requests.exceptions.Timeout as errt:
        print("Timeout Error:", errt)
    except requests.exceptions.RequestException as err:
        print("Something went wrong:", err)

# Fetch the JSON data
data = fetch_data_with_session(url, headers)

# Extract data for plotting if available
if data:
    records = data.get('data', [])
    if records:
        # Sort records by 'CH_TIMESTAMP' to ensure dates
are in ascending order
        sorted_records = sorted(records, key=lambda x:
x.get("CH_TIMESTAMP", ""))

        # Extract the sorted data into lists for plotting
        timestamps = [record.get("CH_TIMESTAMP", "") for
record in sorted_records]
        closing_prices = [record.get("CH_CLOSING_PRICE",
0) for record in sorted_records]
        vwap_values = [record.get("VWAP", 0) for record in
sorted_records]

        # Create a line plot
        plt.figure(figsize=(10, 5))
        plt.plot(timestamps, closing_prices, marker='o',
label='Close Price', color='blue')
        plt.plot(timestamps, vwap_values, marker='x',
label='VWAP', color='red')

        # Set the x-axis and y-axis labels
        plt.xlabel('Date')
        plt.ylabel('Price')
        plt.title('ITC Closing Price and VWAP Over Time')
```

```python
        # Rotate x-axis labels for better readability
        plt.xticks(rotation=45, ha='right')

        # Display a legend to differentiate between lines
        plt.legend()

        # Show the plot
        plt.tight_layout()
        plt.show()
    else:
        print("No records available.")
else:
    print("No data available or failed to fetch data.")
```

<u>Note:</u>

In this the essential explanation for the codes are given as comments. It can be suitably modified based on the needs. The requests library in Python is used for making HTTP requests, such as GET and POST requests, to interact with APIs or download content from the internet. It simplifies making web requests and handling responses, such as fetching JSON data from a URL.

Why Use requests?

**Simplified syntax**: Makes it easier to send HTTP/1.1 requests, with a user-friendly interface.

**Automatic Decoding**: Automatically decodes content (like JSON) based on headers.

**Handles Errors**: Can easily handle HTTP errors and connection issues with built-in methods.

Output of the graph is shown below:

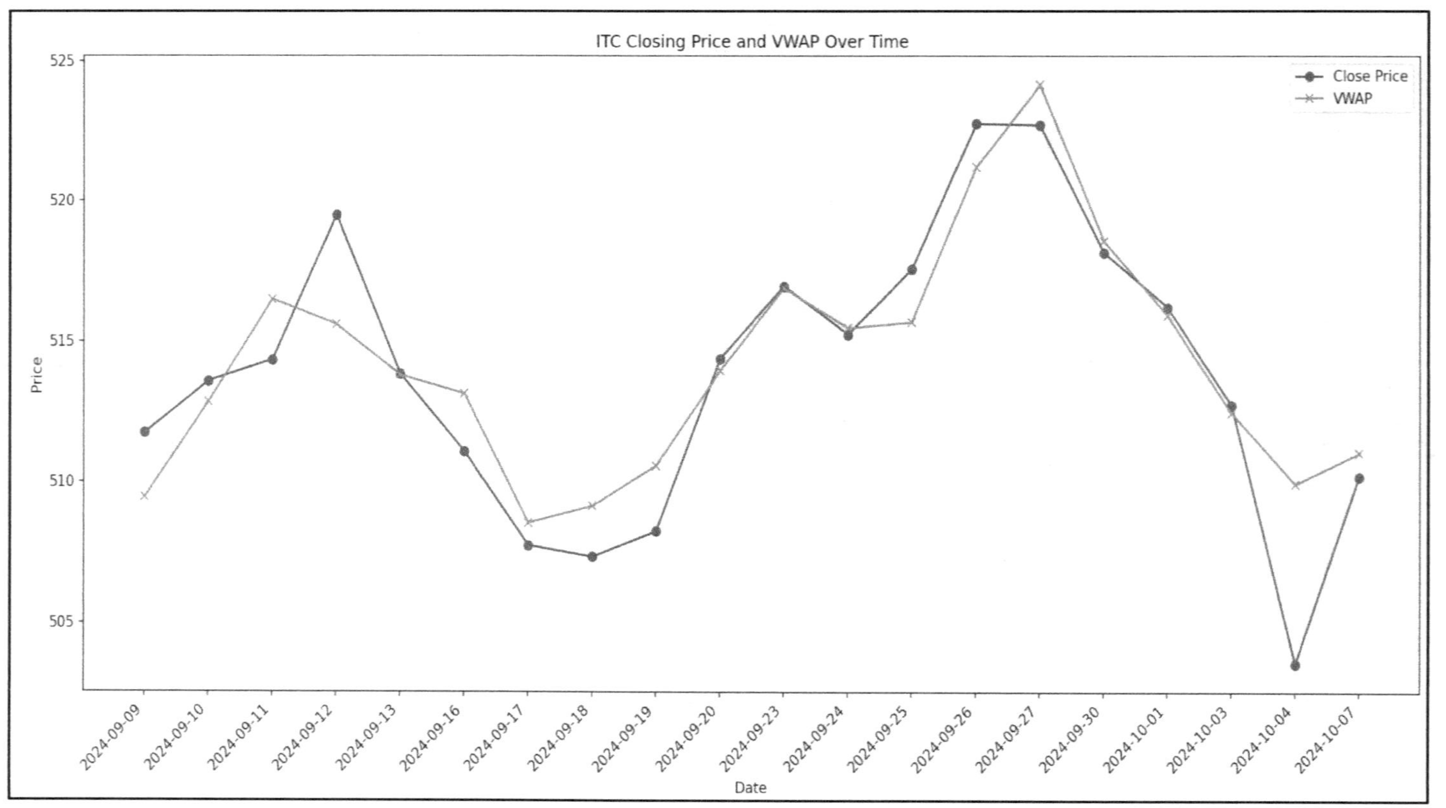

ITC Closing Price and VWAP Over Time
Close Price
VWAP
Price
525
520
515
510
505
2024-09-09
2024-09-10
2024-09-11
2024-09-12
2024-09-13
2024-09-16
2024-09-17
2024-09-18
2024-09-19
2024-09-20
2024-09-23
2024-09-24
2024-09-25
2024-09-26
2024-09-27
2024-09-30
2024-10-01
2024-10-03
2024-10-04
2024-10-07
Date

## 9. Extracting historical data from .csv file

Historical data of an equity or index can be easily obtained from NSE website. The .csv file contains various data and following code can extract the required data. Unlike JSON link, this is straightforward method without errors related to blocking.

Following code demonstrates the extraction of 1 year data for the equity TCS. The data can be downloaded as .csv and the required data can be fetched.

Go to NSE India website and search the equity (TCS).

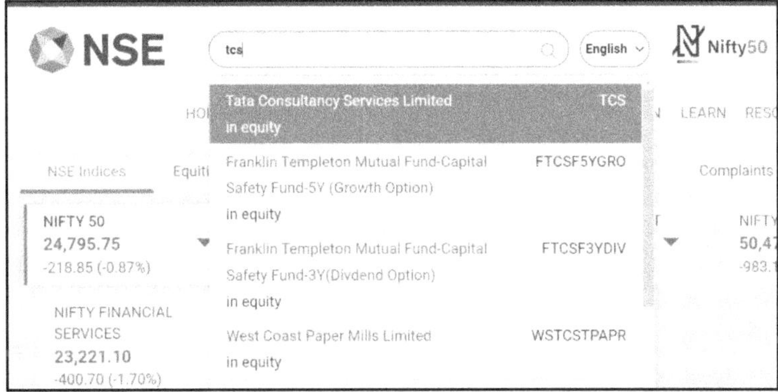

Select Historical Data.

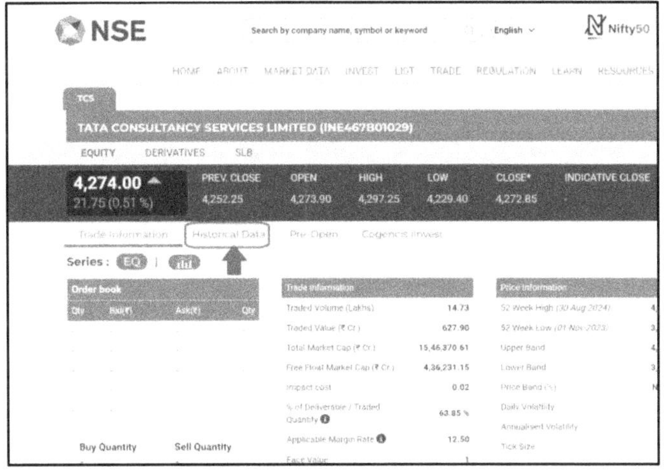

Then select 1Y (one year) or the required dates.

Select Series as EQ (equity) and download the .csv file.

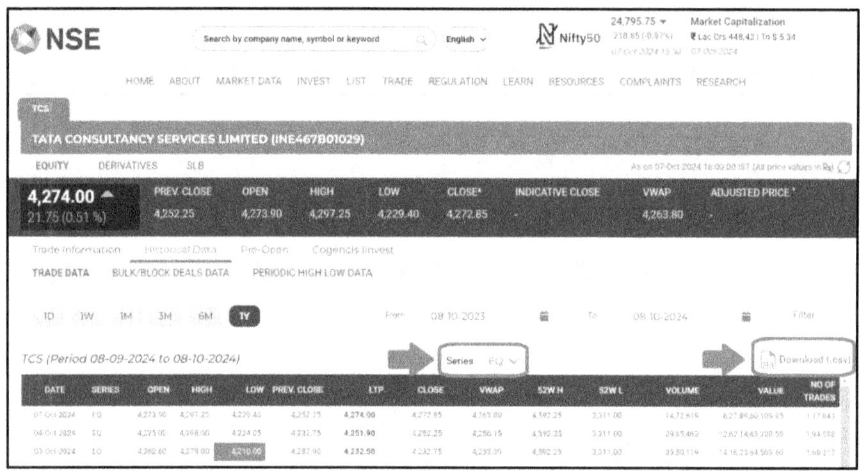

This .csv file contains many values such as "Date ","series ","OPEN ","HIGH ","LOW ","PREV. CLOSE ","ltp ","close ","vwap ","52W H ","52W L ","VOLUME ","VALUE ","No of trades " for the selected equity. The required data from this can be fetched for further analysis with the following code.

For this demonstration, the downloaded file is saved in Desktop as TCS.csv. And it must be emphasized that, the data is in the descending order of the dates and this code sorts the date in ascending order and the relevant Close price data from column 8 of .csv file.

<u>Code</u>
```python
import csv
from datetime import datetime

# File path
file_path = r"C:\Users\...\Desktop\TCS.csv"

# Initialize lists to store date and relevant column data
dates = []
column_8_data = []

# Read the CSV file
with open(file_path, 'r') as file:
    reader = csv.reader(file)
    next(reader)  # Skip the header if there is one
    for row in reader:
        # Convert the date string to a datetime object using the correct format
        date = datetime.strptime(row[0], '%d-%b-%Y')   # Adjusted to match '07-Oct-2024' format
        dates.append(date)
        column_8_data.append(row[7])  # Python uses 0-based indexing, so 7 is the 8th column

# Combine and sort data by dates in ascending order
sorted_data = sorted(zip(dates, column_8_data))

# Print the sorted data with serial numbers
for index, (date, data) in enumerate(sorted_data, start=1):
    print(f"{index}.          {date.strftime('%d-%b-%Y')} {data}")
```

## Output

Data is for 248 dates, sorted in the ascending order of the dates.

```
Python 3.11.3 (tags/v3.11.3:f3909b8, Apr  4 2023, 23:49:59)
AMD64)] on win32
Type "help", "copyright", "credits" or "license()" for more
>>>
==================== RESTART: C:\Users\█████\Desktop\TCS.py
1.  09-Oct-2023    3,638.35
2.  10-Oct-2023    3,628.90
3.  11-Oct-2023    3,609.90
4.  12-Oct-2023    3,542.55
5.  13-Oct-2023    3,570.85
6.  16-Oct-2023    3,524.05
7.  17-Oct-2023    3,507.05
8.  18-Oct-2023    3,487.25
9.  19-Oct-2023    3,455.65
10. 20-Oct-2023    3,494.55
11. 23-Oct-2023    3,410.15
12. 25-Oct-2023    3,390.10
13. 26-Oct-2023    3,336.75
14. 27-Oct-2023    3,350.95
15. 30-Oct-2023    3,378.55
16. 31-Oct-2023    3,368.75
17. 01-Nov-2023    3,330.65
18. 02-Nov-2023    3,360.10
19. 03-Nov-2023    3,350.90
20. 06-Nov-2023    3,380.25
21. 07-Nov-2023    3,370.45
22. 08-Nov-2023    3,381.55
23. 09-Nov-2023    3,347.45
24. 10-Nov-2023    3,333.45
25. 12-Nov-2023    3,357.30
26. 13-Nov-2023    3,331.55
27. 15-Nov-2023    3,404.30
28. 16-Nov-2023    3,497.85

231. 11-Sep-2024    4,479.35
232. 12-Sep-2024    4,517.70
233. 13-Sep-2024    4,522.60
234. 16-Sep-2024    4,513.25
235. 17-Sep-2024    4,505.65
236. 18-Sep-2024    4,346.15
237. 19-Sep-2024    4,296.15
238. 20-Sep-2024    4,284.90
239. 23-Sep-2024    4,268.50
240. 24-Sep-2024    4,271.30
241. 25-Sep-2024    4,274.75
242. 26-Sep-2024    4,292.50
243. 27-Sep-2024    4,308.70
244. 30-Sep-2024    4,268.50
245. 01-Oct-2024    4,287.90
246. 03-Oct-2024    4,232.75
247. 04-Oct-2024    4,252.25
248. 07-Oct-2024    4,272.85
>>>
```

# 10. Calculating Simple Moving Average (SMA)

## 10.1 Basics of SMA

Calculating the moving average is important to predict the price trend and trend reversal. Simple moving average (SMA) is a stable technical indicator and it is based on calculation of the average price of an equity over a given period of time, say consecutive 20-days.

To calculate the SMA, generally closing prices are summed-up for the given period (in specific number of days) and divide the sum by the number of days. For example, to calculate 10-day SMA, closing prices of consecutive 10 days are added and the net value is divided by 10.

If a short-term SMA crosses below a long-term SMA, it is called as death cross and this indicates a bearish trend and the price of the equity may be further in downtrend. When a short-term SMA crosses above a long-term SMA, it is called a golden cross and this indicates a bullish breakout pattern. This means that the price is likely to turn upward.

Following code is based the equity TCS. One-year historical prices of TCS data is download from the NSE website and the downloaded file is saved in Desktop as TCS.csv.

It must be emphasized that, the data is in the descending order of the dates and this code sorts the date in ascending order and the relevant Close price data from column 8. Then 5-day and

30-day SMA values are calculated and printed. Further a line graph is plotted between the Date against Close price, 5-day SMA and 30-day SMA using Matplotlib.

## 10.2 Illustration with price data of TCS

Following example demonstrates the 5-day and 30-day SMA for the 1-year price data of TCS.

| # | Date | Close Price | 5-day SMA | 30-day SMA |
|---|---|---|---|---|
| 1 | 09-Oct-23 | 3638.35 | | |
| 2 | 10-Oct-23 | 3628.90 | | |
| 3 | 11-Oct-23 | 3609.90 | | |
| 4 | 12-Oct-23 | 3542.55 | | |
| 5 | 13-Oct-23 | 3570.85 | 3598.11 | |
| 6 | 16-Oct-23 | 3524.05 | 3575.25 | |
| 7 | 17-Oct-23 | 3507.05 | 3550.88 | |
| 8 | 18-Oct-23 | 3487.25 | 3526.35 | |
| 9 | 19-Oct-23 | 3455.65 | 3508.97 | |
| 10 | 20-Oct-23 | 3494.55 | 3493.71 | |
| 11 | 23-Oct-23 | 3410.15 | 3470.93 | |
| 12 | 25-Oct-23 | 3390.10 | 3447.54 | |
| 13 | 26-Oct-23 | 3336.75 | 3417.44 | |
| 14 | 27-Oct-23 | 3350.95 | 3396.50 | |
| 15 | 30-Oct-23 | 3378.55 | 3373.30 | |
| 16 | 31-Oct-23 | 3368.75 | 3365.02 | |
| 17 | 01-Nov-23 | 3330.65 | 3353.13 | |
| 18 | 02-Nov-23 | 3360.10 | 3357.80 | |
| 19 | 03-Nov-23 | 3350.90 | 3357.79 | |
| 20 | 06-Nov-23 | 3380.25 | 3358.13 | |
| 21 | 07-Nov-23 | 3370.45 | 3358.47 | |
| 22 | 08-Nov-23 | 3381.55 | 3368.65 | |
| 23 | 09-Nov-23 | 3347.45 | 3366.12 | |

| 24 | 10-Nov-23 | 3333.45 | 3362.63 | |
|---|---|---|---|---|
| 25 | 12-Nov-23 | 3357.30 | 3358.04 | |
| 26 | 13-Nov-23 | 3331.55 | 3350.26 | |
| 27 | 15-Nov-23 | 3404.30 | 3354.81 | |
| 28 | 16-Nov-23 | 3497.85 | 3384.89 | |
| 29 | 17-Nov-23 | 3502.45 | 3418.69 | |
| 30 | 20-Nov-23 | 3519.60 | 3451.15 | 3438.74 |
| 31 | 21-Nov-23 | 3510.20 | 3486.88 | 3434.47 |
| 32 | 22-Nov-23 | 3530.15 | 3512.05 | 3431.18 |
| 33 | 23-Nov-23 | 3508.25 | 3514.13 | 3427.79 |
| 34 | 24-Nov-23 | 3457.10 | 3505.06 | 3424.94 |
| 35 | 28-Nov-23 | 3470.15 | 3495.17 | 3421.58 |
| 36 | 29-Nov-23 | 3513.75 | 3495.88 | 3421.24 |

And the relevant code for this 5-day SMA and 30-day SMA based on Close Price is given below:

**Code**

```python
import csv
from datetime import datetime
import matplotlib.pyplot as plt

# File path
file_path = r"C:\Users\...\Desktop\TCS.csv"

# Initialize lists to store date and relevant column data
dates = []
close_prices = []

# Read the CSV file
with open(file_path, 'r') as file:
    reader = csv.reader(file)
    next(reader)  # Skip the header if there is one
    for row in reader:
        # Convert the date string to a datetime object using
the correct format
        date = datetime.strptime(row[0], '%d-%b-%Y')

# Adjusted to match '07-Oct-2024' format
```

```python
# Remove commas and convert the close price to a float
        close_price = float(row[7].replace(',', ''))
        dates.append(date)
        close_prices.append(close_price)

# Combine and sort data by dates in ascending order
sorted_data = sorted(zip(dates, close_prices))
dates_sorted, close_prices_sorted = zip(*sorted_data)

# Calculate the 5-day and 30-day moving averages
def moving_average(data, window_size):
    return        [round(sum(data[i:i+window_size])       /
window_size, 2) for i in range(len(data) - window_size +
1)]

# Compute moving averages
ma_5 = [None] * 4 + moving_average(close_prices_sorted, 5)
# Padding None for first 4 values
ma_30 = [None] * 29 + moving_average(close_prices_sorted,
30)  # Padding None for first 29 values

# Print the sorted data along with serial numbers, close
price, 5-day and 30-day moving averages
print("S.No    Date                Close Price    5-Day MA    30-
Day MA")
for     index,    (date,    price,    ma5,    ma30)    in
enumerate(zip(dates_sorted,   close_prices_sorted,   ma_5,
ma_30), start=1):
    print(f"{index:<5}          {date.strftime('%d-%b-%Y')}
{price:.2f}   {ma5 if ma5 is not None else ''}   {ma30 if
ma30 is not None else ''}")

# Plot the line graph
plt.figure(figsize=(10, 6))
plt.plot(dates_sorted,                  close_prices_sorted,
linestyle='dashed',   linewidth=1,   label='Close    Price',
color='black')
plt.plot(dates_sorted,    ma_5,    label='5-Day    MA',
color='blue')
plt.plot(dates_sorted,    ma_30,    label='30-Day    MA',
color='red')

# Customize the plot
plt.xlabel('Date')
plt.ylabel('Price')
```

```python
plt.title('TCS Stock Close Price and Moving Averages')
plt.legend()
plt.grid(True)
plt.xticks(rotation=45)
plt.tight_layout()

# Display the plot
plt.show()
```

## Screenshots of the output

```
>>>
==================== RESTART: C:\Users\MKS\Desktop\TCS.py ==
S.No    Date          Close Price   5-Day MA   30-Day MA
1       09-Oct-2023   3638.35
2       10-Oct-2023   3628.90
3       11-Oct-2023   3609.90
4       12-Oct-2023   3542.55
5       13-Oct-2023   3570.85      3598.11
6       16-Oct-2023   3524.05      3575.25
7       17-Oct-2023   3507.05      3550.88
8       18-Oct-2023   3487.25      3526.35
9       19-Oct-2023   3455.65      3508.97
10      20-Oct-2023   3494.55      3493.71
11      23-Oct-2023   3410.15      3470.93
12      25-Oct-2023   3390.10      3447.54
13      26-Oct-2023   3336.75      3417.44
14      27-Oct-2023   3350.95      3396.5
15      30-Oct-2023   3378.55      3373.3
16      31-Oct-2023   3368.75      3365.02
17      01-Nov-2023   3330.65      3353.13
18      02-Nov-2023   3360.10      3357.8
19      03-Nov-2023   3350.90      3357.79
20      06-Nov-2023   3380.25      3358.13
21      07-Nov-2023   3370.45      3358.47
22      08-Nov-2023   3381.55      3368.65
23      09-Nov-2023   3347.45      3366.12     |
24      10-Nov-2023   3333.45      3362.63
25      12-Nov-2023   3357.30      3358.04
26      13-Nov-2023   3331.55      3350.26
27      15-Nov-2023   3404.30      3354.81
28      16-Nov-2023   3497.85      3384.89
29      17-Nov-2023   3502.45      3418.69
30      20-Nov-2023   3519.60      3451.15     3438.74
31      21-Nov-2023   3510.20      3486.88     3434.47
32      22-Nov-2023   3530.15      3512.05     3431.18
33      23-Nov-2023   3508.25      3514.13     3427.79
34      24-Nov-2023   3457.10      3505.06     3424.94
35      28-Nov-2023   3470.15      3495.17     3421.58
36      29-Nov-2023   3513.75      3495.88     3421.24
```

The output of the graph is shown below:

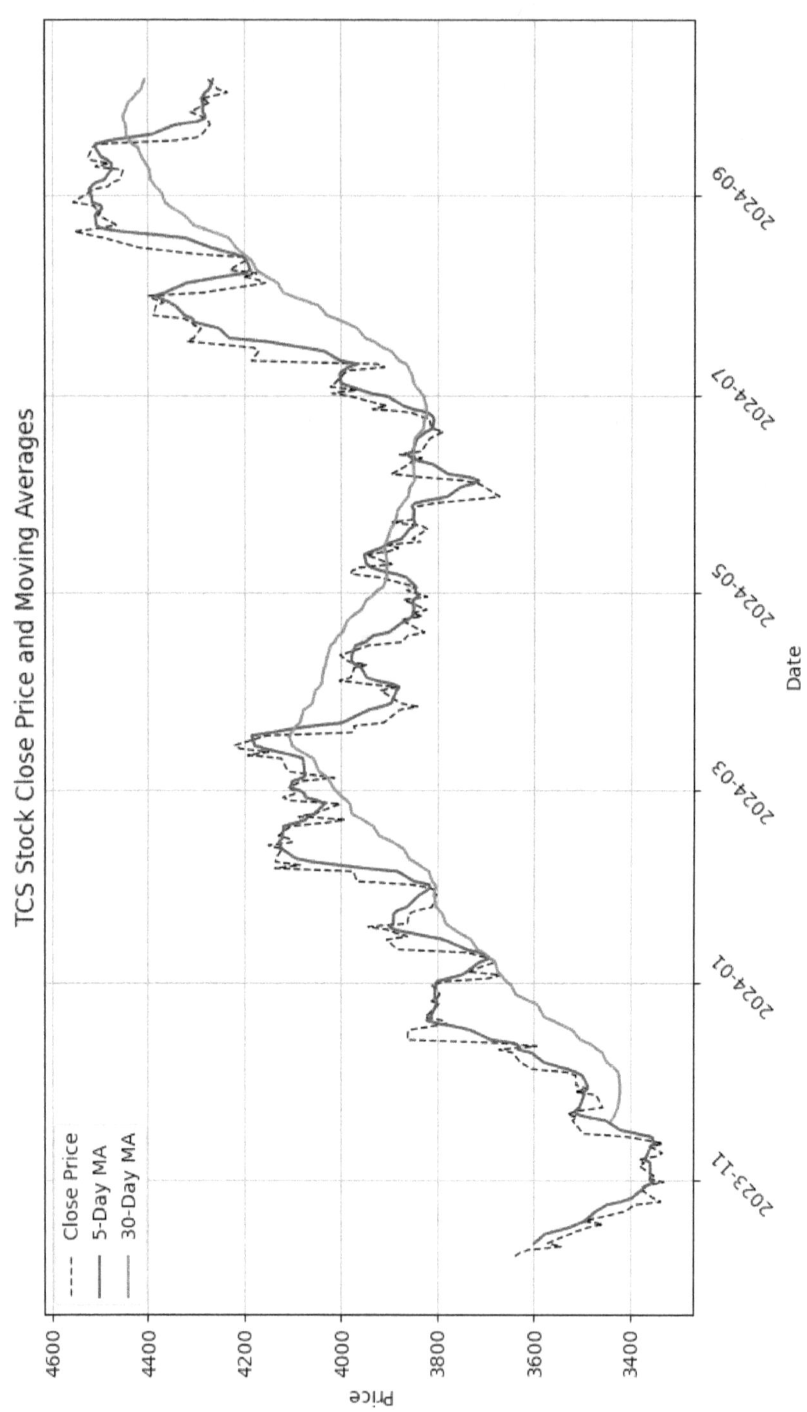


TCS Stock Close Price and Moving Averages
Close Price
5-Day MA
30-Day MA
Price
Date
4600
4400
4200
4000
3800
3600
3400
2023-11
2024-01
2024-03
2024-05
2024-07
2024-09

## 11. Automating the data fetching

Generally, most of the JSON link files are associated with the stock symbols as a part. For example, for the equity State Bank of India the associated JSON link for the price info is:

https://www.nseindia.com/api/quote-equity?symbol=SBIN

If the symbol (here SBIN) is replaced with TCS then the data for Tata Consultancy Services can be fetched.

To achieve this, a list of symbols for which the data is required should be listed one by one in a text file. For this demonstration, six Bank NIFTY stocks are selected and the symbols are stored in a text file and saved in Desktop as:

C:\Users\...\Desktop\BN.txt

Following six stock symbols from Bank NIFTY are listed one by one in the BN.txt file as:

```
HDFCBANK
ICICIBANK
SBIN
KOTAKBANK
AXISBANK
INDUSINDBK
```

Now by using the following JSON link, monthly closing prices for all these stocks should be fetched:

https://www.nseindia.com/api/historical/cm/equity?symbol={B}

where the value of 'B' is replaced by the symbol one by one through the iteration process, by fetching from the BN.txt file.

## 11.1 Possible errors

<u>Manual download</u>

Due to IP blocking by NSE for multiple requests for JSON file, it is advisable to download the individual JSON file for the equity and stored in a separate folder. And each JSON file is named with the stock symbol. Instead of NSE web hyperlink for JSON, this folder path can be used.

<u>IP Blocking</u>

When the script remains idle for a long time and does not provide any output, it may be due to that the NSE website is blocking automated requests, even when using a session and appropriate headers. The NSE website has strict measures for preventing scraping and automated access. So, if error occurs, it is due to the blocking the web scrapping by multiple requests.

After a delay, it may fetch the data. It can be done by 'delay between requests'. For this, a time.sleep(2) can be included between each request to avoid the rate-limiting of the server.

It is convenient to download the respective JSON files in the local directory to avoid such errors.

**Code**
```
import requests
# fetching monthly close prices

# Path to the BN.txt file
bn_file_path = r"C:\Users\...\Desktop\BN.txt"

# Read stock symbols from BN.txt
with open(bn_file_path, 'r') as file:
```

```python
    stock_symbols = [line.strip() for line in
file.readlines()]

# Function to fetch and print data for each stock symbol
def fetch_stock_data(symbol):
    url =
f"https://www.nseindia.com/api/historical/cm/equity?symbo
l={symbol}"
    headers = {
        "User-Agent": "Mozilla/5.0"
    }

    try:
        response = requests.get(url, headers=headers)
        data = response.json()

        # Print the CH_SYMBOL once as a heading
        ch_symbol = data.get('data')[0].get('CH_SYMBOL',
'Symbol Not Found')
        print(f"{ch_symbol}")
        print("Date Close Price")

        # Extract and print Date and Close Price
        for record in data.get('data', []):
            date = record.get('CH_TIMESTAMP', 'N/A')
            close_price = record.get('CH_CLOSING_PRICE',
'N/A')

            print(f"{date} {close_price}")

        # Print a line break between stocks
        print("\n")

    except Exception as e:
        print(f"Error fetching data for {symbol}: {e}")

# Iterate over each stock symbol and fetch data
for stock in stock_symbols:
    fetch_stock_data(stock)


# Note: May shows errors, or waiting to fetch the data for
long time or no data may be fetched due to a block by NSE
for such multiple data requests.
```

## Output

```
HDFCBANK
Date            Close Price
09-10-2024      1633.15
08-10-2024      1651.05
07-10-2024      1617.8
04-10-2024      1657.65
03-10-2024      1682
01-10-2024      1726.2
30-09-2024      1732.05
27-09-2024      1752.65
26-09-2024      1783.45
25-09-2024      1779.1
24-09-2024      1768.05
23-09-2024      1759.8
20-09-2024      1741.2
19-09-2024      1708.5
18-09-2024      1694.8
17-09-2024      1668.8
16-09-2024      1670.95
13-09-2024      1665.95
12-09-2024      1666.6
11-09-2024      1643.9
10-09-2024      1650.35

ICICIBANK
Date            Close Price
09-10-2024      1244.15
08-10-2024      1236.6
07-10-2024      1233.9
04-10-2024      1239.75
03-10-2024      1256.35
01-10-2024      1274.4
30-09-2024      1273
27-09-2024      1306.6
26-09-2024      1329.05
25-09-2024      1323.85
24-09-2024      1318.6
23-09-2024      1321.9
20-09-2024      1338.45
19-09-2024      1292
18-09-2024      1288.35
17-09-2024      1268.1
```

| | |
|---|---|
| 16-09-2024 | 1262.85 |
| 13-09-2024 | 1250.35 |
| 12-09-2024 | 1252.15 |
| 11-09-2024 | 1236.35 |
| 10-09-2024 | 1237.3 |

SBIN

| Date | Close Price |
|---|---|
| 09-10-2024 | 797.4 |
| 08-10-2024 | 781.45 |
| 07-10-2024 | 770.65 |
| 04-10-2024 | 796.65 |
| 03-10-2024 | 794.1 |
| 01-10-2024 | 796.95 |
| 30-09-2024 | 787.9 |
| 27-09-2024 | 802.65 |
| 26-09-2024 | 801.85 |
| 25-09-2024 | 793.1 |
| 24-09-2024 | 798.25 |
| 23-09-2024 | 801.85 |
| 20-09-2024 | 781.7 |
| 19-09-2024 | 789.95 |
| 18-09-2024 | 792.75 |
| 17-09-2024 | 782.9 |
| 16-09-2024 | 785.55 |
| 13-09-2024 | 790.85 |
| 12-09-2024 | 787.75 |
| 11-09-2024 | 768.6 |
| 10-09-2024 | 782.65 |

KOTAKBANK

| Date | Close Price |
|---|---|
| 09-10-2024 | 1800.8 |
| 08-10-2024 | 1803.4 |
| 07-10-2024 | 1790.25 |
| 04-10-2024 | 1809 |
| 03-10-2024 | 1822.8 |
| 01-10-2024 | 1879.4 |
| 30-09-2024 | 1853.95 |
| 27-09-2024 | 1872.45 |
| 26-09-2024 | 1902.3 |
| 25-09-2024 | 1897.95 |
| 24-09-2024 | 1914.7 |
| 23-09-2024 | 1934.7 |
| 20-09-2024 | 1904.5 |

```
19-09-2024        1871.95
18-09-2024        1839.7
17-09-2024        1846.65
16-09-2024        1831.3
13-09-2024        1820.35
12-09-2024        1827.45
11-09-2024        1789.25
10-09-2024        1791.6

AXISBANK
Date              Close Price
09-10-2024        1170.15
08-10-2024        1153.3
07-10-2024        1145.7
04-10-2024        1178.4
03-10-2024        1175.7
01-10-2024        1226.65
30-09-2024        1232.2
27-09-2024        1273.15
26-09-2024        1277.1
25-09-2024        1268.1
24-09-2024        1239.55
23-09-2024        1246.8
20-09-2024        1245
19-09-2024        1242.7
18-09-2024        1240.45
17-09-2024        1232.1
16-09-2024        1231.05
13-09-2024        1217.45
12-09-2024        1203.35
11-09-2024        1186.1
10-09-2024        1187.2

INDUSINDBK
Date              Close Price
09-10-2024        1341.55
08-10-2024        1359.55
07-10-2024        1350.85
04-10-2024        1382.85
03-10-2024        1387.75
01-10-2024        1409.7
30-09-2024        1447.6
27-09-2024        1462.7
26-09-2024        1452.7
25-09-2024        1439.5
```

| Date | Price |
|------|-------|
| 24-09-2024 | 1448.3 |
| 23-09-2024 | 1465.1 |
| 20-09-2024 | 1480.2 |
| 19-09-2024 | 1484.75 |
| 18-09-2024 | 1480.25 |
| 17-09-2024 | 1466.35 |
| 16-09-2024 | 1470.2 |
| 13-09-2024 | 1464.05 |
| 12-09-2024 | 1443.35 |
| 11-09-2024 | 1421.2 |
| 10-09-2024 | 1435.55 |

## 12. Importing the fetched data as .csv file

It is convenient to store the fetched data in a spreadsheet format for further analysis, future reference as well as for graph plotting. And the algorithm is similar to the previous method.

For this, six Bank NIFTY stocks are selected and the symbols are stored in a text file and saved in Desktop as:

C:\Users\...\Desktop\BN.txt

Following six stock symbols from Bank NIFTY are listed one by one in the BN.txt file as:

```
HDFCBANK
ICICIBANK
SBIN
KOTAKBANK
AXISBANK
INDUSINDBK
```

Now by using the following JSON link, monthly closing prices for all these stocks should be fetched:

https://www.nseindia.com/api/historical/cm/equity?symbol={B}

where the value of 'B' is replaced by the symbol one by one through the iteration process, by fetching from the BN.txt file.

After fetching the close price data against the date under each equity symbol, is stored as .csv file with the file name BN.csv in the same path location, where the Python module is kept.

As previously explained, this process may show errors, or waiting to fetch the data for long time or no data may be fetched due to a block by NSE for multiple requests.

## Code

```python
import requests
import csv

# Path to the BN.txt file
bn_file_path = r"C:\Users\...\Desktop\BN.txt"
# Path to save the BN.csv file
csv_file_path = r"C:\Users\...\Desktop\BN.csv"

# Read stock symbols from BN.txt
with open(bn_file_path, 'r') as file:
    stock_symbols   =   [line.strip()   for   line   in
file.readlines()]

# Open the CSV file for writing
with open(csv_file_path, 'w', newline='') as csvfile:
    csv_writer = csv.writer(csvfile)

    # Iterate over each stock symbol and fetch data
    for stock in stock_symbols:
        url                                              =
f"https://www.nseindia.com/api/historical/cm/equity?symbo
l={stock}"
        headers = {
            "User-Agent": "Mozilla/5.0"
        }

        try:
            response = requests.get(url, headers=headers)
            data = response.json()

            # Write the stock symbol as a heading
            ch_symbol                                    =
data.get('data')[0].get('CH_SYMBOL', 'Symbol Not Found')
            csv_writer.writerow([ch_symbol])     #   Write
stock symbol as a row
            csv_writer.writerow(["Date",  "Close  Price"])
# Write the headers for each stock

            # Extract and write Date and Close Price
            for record in data.get('data', []):
                date = record.get('CH_TIMESTAMP', 'N/A')
                close_price                              =
record.get('CH_CLOSING_PRICE', 'N/A')
                csv_writer.writerow([date, close_price])
```

```
        # Write an empty row between stocks
        csv_writer.writerow([])

    except Exception as e:
        print(f"Error fetching data for {stock}: {e}")
```

### <u>Output</u>

BN.csv file is created in Desktop and the Dates and the corresponding Close Prices data for one-month are stored in two columns under each stock symbol. Data values for each equity is separated by an empty row.

## 13. Fetching the price data for multiple stocks

Price data for equities under different indices are available at:

https://www.nseindia.com/market-data/live-equity-market

Select the required Index and the Price data for the equity components will be loaded. Identify the relevant JSON file link.

To avoid the blocking and restricting the multiple time access by NSE, it is better to download the JSON file.

Following code illustrates fetching the close price data for stock components listed under NIFTY 100 and the corresponding JSON file link is:

https://www.nseindia.com/api/equity-

stockIndices?index=NIFTY%20100

And this JSON file is downloaded and saved with the filename NIFTY100, in the following path:

C:\Users\...\Desktop\NIFTY100.json

This code fetches the data for Symbol, Last Traded Price, 1-month Price Change (%) and 1-year Price Change (%).

Finally, the data is sorted in the descending order of the 1-year return to correlate the growth.

Price data as on 10-10-2024.

**<u>Code</u>**

```python
import json

# Path to the JSON file
file_path = r"C:\Users\...\Desktop\NIFTY100.json"
```

```python
# Load the JSON data
with open(file_path, 'r') as file:
    data = json.load(file)

# Extract the stock data from the "data" key
stocks_data = data.get("data", [])

# Convert the 'perChange365d' values to float for sorting,
handling cases where it's not available
for stock in stocks_data:
    # Attempt to convert 'perChange365d' to a float, using
-inf for missing or invalid values
    try:
        stock["perChange365d"]                            =
float(stock.get("perChange365d", "-inf"))
    except ValueError:
        stock["perChange365d"] = float("-inf")

# Sort the stocks data in descending order based on
'perChange365d'
stocks_data_sorted  =  sorted(stocks_data,  key=lambda  x:
x["perChange365d"], reverse=True)

# Print the headers
print(f"{'#':<3}  {'Symbol':<10}  {'LTP':<5}  {'1M  Return
(%)':<15} {'1Y Return (%)':<25}")

# Iterate  through  the  sorted  stock  data  and  print  the
required data
for index, stock in enumerate(stocks_data_sorted, start=1):
    if isinstance(stock, dict):
        symbol = stock.get("symbol", "N/A")
        last_price = stock.get("lastPrice", "N/A")
        change_30d = stock.get("perChange30d", "N/A")
        change_365d = stock.get("perChange365d", "N/A")

        print(f"{index:<3}  {symbol:<10}  {last_price:<10}
{change_30d:<15} {change_365d:<10}")
    else:
        print(f"{index:<3}    Unexpected    data    format:
{stock}")
```

# Python codes to fetch & analyze NSE stock market data

## <u>Output (Snippet)</u>

| #  | Symbol     | LTP      | 1M Return (%) | 1Y Return (%) |
|----|------------|----------|---------------|---------------|
| 1  | BAJAJ-AUTO | 11890    | 7.68          | 133.63        |
| 2  | MOTHERSON  | 210.28   | 10.77         | 120.15        |
| 3  | BHEL       | 269.7    | 2.59          | 107.37        |
| 4  | IRFC       | 151.38   | -10.79        | 100.3         |
| 5  | NAUKRI     | 8285.05  | 10.95         | 94.48         |
| 6  | BOSCHLTD   | 38360.5  | 13.98         | 94.04         |
| 7  | RECLTD     | 539.5    | -5.7          | 86.64         |
| 8  | INDIGO     | 4630.05  | -3.45         | 84.16         |
| 9  | TATAPOWER  | 464.35   | 4.56          | 83.36         |
| 10 | IOC        | 163.98   | -6.36         | 83.27         |
| 11 | HEROMOTOCO | 5460.65  | -3.77         | 75.95         |
| 12 | SHRIRAMFIN | 3334.6   | 2.38          | 75.8          |
| 13 | ADANIPORTS | 1412.65  | -2.49         | 73.92         |
| 14 | NHPC       | 90.39    | -4.46         | 72.81         |
| 15 | SUNPHARMA  | 1893.15  | 2.8           | 67.24         |
| 16 | COALINDIA  | 488.65   | -0.61         | 61.7          |
| 17 | ICICIGI    | 2082.6   | -3.75         | 58.35         |
| 18 | LICI       | 968      | -6.49         | 51.43         |
| 19 | HINDALCO   | 736.7    | 10.71         | 50.89         |
| 20 | TATAMOTORS | 931.65   | -10.36        | 46.45         |
| 21 | LODHA      | 1177     | -0.34         | 45.44         |
| 22 | JINDALSTEL | 992.95   | 2.99          | 43.06         |
| 23 | ICICIPRULI | 740.6    | -0.05         | 42.05         |
| 24 | CIPLA      | 1577.15  | -0.8          | 38.14         |
| 25 | ULTRACEMCO | 11415.65 | -0.96         | 37.0          |
| 26 | PNB        | 103.84   | -5.38         | 36.34         |
| 27 | SBIN       | 796.55   | 1.85          | 35.48         |
| 28 | EICHERMOT  | 4688.75  | -0.83         | 34.74         |

## 14. OPEN HIGH OPEN LOW (OHOL) strategy

In the intra-day, if the Open price of a stock is equal to intra-day High price, then it indicates the bearish trend and if the Open price of a stock is equal to intra-day low price, then it indicates the bullish trend.

Price data for equities under different indices are available at:

https://www.nseindia.com/market-data/live-equity-market

Select the required Index and the Price data for the equity components will be loaded. Identify the relevant JSON file link.

To avoid the blocking and restricting the multiple time access by NSE, it is better to download the JSON file.

Following code illustrates OHOL strategy to identify bearish as well as bullish stocks from NIFTY 500 components and the corresponding JSON file link is:

https://www.nseindia.com/api/equity-stockIndices?index=NIFTY%20500

And this JSON file is downloaded and saved with the filename NIFTY500, in the following path:

C:\Users\...\Desktop\NIFTY500.json

Price data as on 10-10-2024.

**<u>Code</u>**
```python
import json

# Load the JSON data from the file
file_path = r'C:\Users\...\Desktop\NIFTY500.json'
```

```python
with open(file_path, 'r') as file:
    data = json.load(file)

# Check if the JSON structure contains a list or a nested
structure.
# Adjust the following line if your stock data is nested
under a specific key.
stocks = data.get('data', data)  # Replace 'data' with the
correct key if needed.


# Iterate over each stock and perform the comparison
for stock in stocks:
    if isinstance(stock, dict):
        symbol = stock.get('symbol', 'Unknown Symbol')
        day_high = stock.get('dayHigh')
        day_low = stock.get('dayLow')
        open_price = stock.get('open')

        # Define the status based on the comparison
        if day_high == open_price:
            status = "Bearish"
        elif day_low == open_price:
            status = "Bullish"
        else:
            continue  # Skip if neither condition is met

        # Print the result in two columns with a distinct
space
        print(f"{symbol:<20} {status}")
```

**<u>Output (Snippet)</u>**

```
NETWORK18            Bullish
360ONE               Bullish
SONATSOFTW           Bullish
PAGEIND              Bullish
NMDC                 Bullish
JINDALSTEL           Bullish
BSOFT                Bullish
METROBRAND           Bullish
NUVAMA               Bullish
ZFCVINDIA            Bullish
SAPPHIRE             Bullish
SBFC                 Bullish
```

| | |
|---|---|
| KIMS | Bullish |
| TECHM | Bullish |
| TITAGARH | Bullish |
| LTIM | Bullish |
| CENTURYPLY | Bullish |
| FEDERALBNK | Bullish |
| ATGL | Bullish |
| INDIANB | Bullish |
| HONAUT | Bearish |
| AAVAS | Bullish |
| WIPRO | Bullish |
| SYNGENE | Bullish |
| VOLTAS | Bearish |
| GLAND | Bearish |
| NESTLEIND | Bearish |
| GODREJCP | Bearish |
| CHALET | Bearish |
| MRF | Bearish |
| ICICIGI | Bearish |
| DELHIVERY | Bearish |
| UCOBANK | Bearish |
| SWSOLAR | Bearish |
| IDBI | Bearish |
| PIDILITIND | Bearish |
| POLYCAB | Bearish |
| KALYANKJIL | Bearish |
| HDFCBANK | Bearish |
| PTCIL | Bearish |
| HAPPSTMNDS | Bearish |
| AFFLE | Bearish |
| TORNTPOWER | Bearish |
| BLUEDART | Bearish |
| GODREJPROP | Bearish |
| AMBER | Bearish |
| INDHOTEL | Bearish |
| DMART | Bearish |
| ICICIPRULI | Bearish |
| CELLO | Bearish |
| CCL | Bearish |
| EQUITASBNK | Bearish |
| VIPIND | Bearish |
| SCHNEIDER | Bearish |
| DLF | Bearish |

# 15. Predicting the trend with price change data

## 15.1 Getting intra-day price change

To get more insight about the day trend of an equity specifically for trading in derivative market, change in the intra-day price should be correlated with the Open price rather than previous day's Close price.

Since the price movements of an equity is news based and also depends on the impact of global market, it is better to correlate the price change with the Open price rather than with previous day's Close price.

It can be analyzed by a simple correlation:

Price change

(%) = (Last traded price - Open price) Open price × 100

This expresses the intra-day price change data in percentage and hence it is a straightforward technique to identify the price trend as strongly bearish or strongly bullish or moderately bearish or moderately bullish.

As already stated, price data for equities under different indices are available at:

https://www.nseindia.com/market-data/live-equity-market

Select the required Index and the Price data for the equity components will be loaded. Identify the relevant JSON file link.

It is accentuated that the data in the JSON is updated in every moment during the live market hours.

To avoid the blocking and restricting the multiple time access by NSE, it is better to download the JSON file.

Following code illustrates the fetching the intra-day price change (%) for equities listed under from NIFTY 500 and the corresponding JSON file link is:

https://www.nseindia.com/api/equity-

stockIndices?index=NIFTY%20500

<u>Screenshot of the beautified JSON file (NETWORK 18)</u>

```
{
  "priority": 0,
  "symbol": "NETWORK18",
  "identifier": "NETWORK18EQN",
  "series": "EQ",
  "open": 76.26,
  "dayHigh": 82,
  "dayLow": 76.26,
  "lastPrice": 81.75,
  "previousClose": 76.26,
  "change": 5.49,
  "pChange": 7.2,
  "totalTradedVolume": 7405699,
  "stockIndClosePrice": null,
  "totalTradedValue": 594603572.71,
  "lastUpdateTime": "11-Oct-2024 15:59:27",
  "yearHigh": 135.7,
  "ffmc": 20444244279.88,
  "yearLow": 65.75,
  "nearWKH": 39.7568165070007,
  "nearWKL": -24.3346007604563,
  "perChange365d": 5.62,
  "date365dAgo": "11-Oct-2023",
  "chart365dPath": "https://nsearchives.nseindia.com/365d/NETWORK18-EQ.svg",
  "date30dAgo": "10-Sep-2024",
  "perChange30d": -15.63,
  "chart30dPath": "https://nsearchives.nseindia.com/30d/NETWORK18-EQ.svg",
  "chartTodayPath": "https://nsearchives.nseindia.com/today/NETWORK18EQN.svg",
```

To get the intra-day price change, data against "open", "lastprice" should be fetched and after the calculation it is stored against the "symbol". Through iterations, price change (%) for every equity should be calculated and sorted in descending order.

<u>Code</u>

```python
import json

# Path to the JSON file
file_path = r"C:\Users\...\Desktop\NIFTY500.json"

# Load the JSON data
try:
    with open(file_path, 'r') as file:
        data = json.load(file)
except json.JSONDecodeError:
    data = {}

# Extract stock data if it's a dictionary containing a list
under a known key
if isinstance(data, dict) and 'data' in data and
isinstance(data['data'], list):
    stocks = data['data']
elif isinstance(data, list):
    stocks = data
else:
    stocks = []

# List to store symbol and its corresponding Price Change
price_changes = []

# Iterate over each stock data
for stock in stocks:
    if isinstance(stock, dict):
        symbol = stock.get("symbol")
        last_price = stock.get("lastPrice")
        open_price = stock.get("open")

        # Ensure values are valid to avoid division errors
        if symbol and last_price is not None and
open_price:
            try:
                # Calculate the price change
                price_change = (last_price - open_price) *
100 / open_price
                price_changes.append((symbol,
price_change))
            except (ZeroDivisionError, TypeError):
                continue
```

```python
# Sort the list by Price Change in descending order
price_changes.sort(key=lambda x: x[1], reverse=True)

# Print the results with serial numbers and spacing
print(f"{'#':<5} {'Symbol':<15} {'Price Change (%)':>20}")
print("=" * 40)
for idx, (symbol, change) in enumerate(price_changes,
start=1):
    print(f"{idx:<5} {symbol:<15} {change:>20.2f}")
```

### Output (Snippet)

| #   | Symbol      | Price Change (%) |
|-----|-------------|-----------------:|
| 1   | USHAMART    | 14.79 |
| 2   | NAM-INDIA   | 8.32 |
| 3   | NETWORK18   | 7.20 |
| 4   | NETWEB      | 6.57 |
| 5   | TRITURBINE  | 6.48 |
| 6   | BSE         | 6.31 |
| 7   | SONATSOFTW  | 6.23 |
| 8   | NUVAMA      | 5.59 |
| 9   | JMFINANCIL  | 5.51 |
| 10  | PERSISTENT  | 5.03 |
| 11  | TV18BRDCST  | 4.91 |
| 12  | DBREALTY    | 4.75 |
| 13  | GMDCLTD     | 4.71 |
| 14  | RAJESHEXPO  | 4.62 |
| 15  | MANKIND     | 4.36 |
| 16  | CRISIL      | 3.88 |
| 17  | NEWGEN      | 3.87 |
| 18  | GRANULES    | 3.87 |
| 19  | OLECTRA     | 3.75 |
| 20  | BANDHANBNK  | 3.68 |
| 21  | SPARC       | 3.63 |
| 22  | MOTILALOFS  | 3.63 |
| 23  | KPITTECH    | 3.56 |
| 24  | SAPPHIRE    | 3.51 |
| 25  | NMDC        | 3.39 |
| 26  | IPCALAB     | 3.38 |
| 27  | ANGELONE    | 3.26 |
| 28  | 360ONE      | 3.19 |
| 29  | JUSTDIAL    | 3.07 |
| 30  | ZFCVINDIA   | 3.06 |

```
.........................................
.........................................
.........................................
```

| 463 | DLF | -1.88 |
| 464 | ALKYLAMINE | -1.93 |
| 465 | JINDALSAW | -1.94 |
| 466 | EMAMILTD | -1.95 |
| 467 | MEDANTA | -1.95 |
| 468 | JUBLPHARMA | -1.96 |
| 469 | MINDACORP | -1.96 |
| 470 | M&M | -1.97 |
| 471 | MAXHEALTH | -1.98 |
| 472 | MAZDOCK | -2.00 |
| 473 | COCHINSHIP | -2.03 |
| 474 | PCBL | -2.05 |
| 475 | ADANIENSOL | -2.11 |
| 476 | EQUITASBNK | -2.16 |
| 477 | POLYMED | -2.16 |
| 478 | AMBER | -2.19 |
| 479 | UNOMINDA | -2.22 |
| 480 | FORTIS | -2.24 |
| 481 | LTF | -2.24 |
| 482 | SUPREMEIND | -2.25 |
| 483 | TTML | -2.27 |
| 484 | ATUL | -2.28 |
| 485 | ISEC | -2.36 |
| 486 | PHOENIXLTD | -2.37 |
| 487 | GRINDWELL | -2.38 |
| 488 | VIPIND | -2.39 |
| 489 | CUMMINSIND | -2.59 |
| 490 | SUNDARMFIN | -2.63 |
| 491 | CREDITACC | -2.70 |
| 492 | WESTLIFE | -2.75 |
| 493 | NBCC | -2.83 |
| 494 | JSWENERGY | -2.97 |
| 495 | STARHEALTH | -2.98 |
| 496 | CROMPTON | -3.14 |
| 497 | JPPOWER | -3.35 |
| 498 | SAREGAMA | -3.58 |
| 499 | ANANDRATHI | -4.14 |
| 500 | IREDA | -4.45 |
| 501 | SWSOLAR | -5.21 |

## 16. Visualizing the intra-day price change with bar chart

It is easy to interpret the intra-day price change data by a graph. Following code gives the bar chart output for the intra-day price change (%) for the data fetched and sorted in the descending order of the price change for NIFTY 500 equities, as given in section 15.

And for the lucidity first and last 5 equities in the sorted list selected (Refer Previous Section 15). JSON file and algorithm are based on the previous Section 15. And only 10 equity data are taken and Matplotlib module is deployed for the plotting.


**Code**
```python
import json
import matplotlib.pyplot as plt

# Path to the JSON file
file_path = r"C:\Users\...\Desktop\NIFTY500.json"


# Load the JSON data
try:
    with open(file_path, 'r') as file:
        data - json.load(file)
except json.JSONDecodeError:
    data = {}

# Extract stock data if it's a dictionary containing a list
under a known key
if isinstance(data, dict) and 'data' in data and
isinstance(data['data'], list):
    stocks = data['data']
elif isinstance(data, list):
    stocks = data
else:
    stocks = []
```

```python
# List to store symbol and its corresponding Price Change
price_changes = []


# Iterate over each stock data
for stock in stocks:
    if isinstance(stock, dict):
        symbol = stock.get("symbol")
        last_price = stock.get("lastPrice")
        open_price = stock.get("open")

        # Ensure values are valid to avoid division errors
        if symbol and last_price is not None and open_price:
            try:
                # Calculate the price change
                price_change = (last_price - open_price) * 100 / open_price
                price_changes.append((symbol, price_change))
            except (ZeroDivisionError, TypeError):
                continue

# Sort the list by Price Change in descending order
price_changes.sort(key=lambda x: x[1], reverse=True)

# Extract the first 5 and last 5 values
top_5 = price_changes[:5]
bottom_5 = price_changes[-5:]

# Combine the two lists for plotting
combined_data = top_5 + bottom_5

# Prepare data for plotting
symbols = [item[0] for item in combined_data]
changes = [item[1] for item in combined_data]

# Create the bar chart
plt.figure(figsize=(10, 6))


# Color bars based on positive or negative change
```

```python
colors = ['blue' if change >= 0 else 'red' for change in
changes]
bars = plt.bar(symbols, changes, color=colors, alpha=0.7)

# Set y-axis limits
plt.ylim(-10, 15)

# Label each bar with the corresponding symbol inside the
bar

for bar, symbol, change in zip(bars, symbols, changes):
    plt.text(
        bar.get_x() + bar.get_width() / 2,
        bar.get_height() / 2,  # Position in the middle of
the bar
        symbol,
        ha='center',
        va='center',
        fontsize=10,
        color='white' if change >= 0 else 'black'  # White
text on blue bars, black on red bars
    )

    # Optionally, label each bar with its percentage value
above or below the bar
    plt.text(
        bar.get_x() + bar.get_width() / 2,
        bar.get_height(),
        f'{change:.2f}%',
        ha='center',
        va='bottom' if change >= 0 else 'top',
        fontsize=10,
        color='black'
    )

# Add labels and title
plt.xlabel('Stock Symbol')
plt.ylabel('Price Change (%)')
plt.title('Intra-day Price Change for Top 5 and Bottom 5
Stocks')
plt.tight_layout()

# Display the plot
plt.show()
```

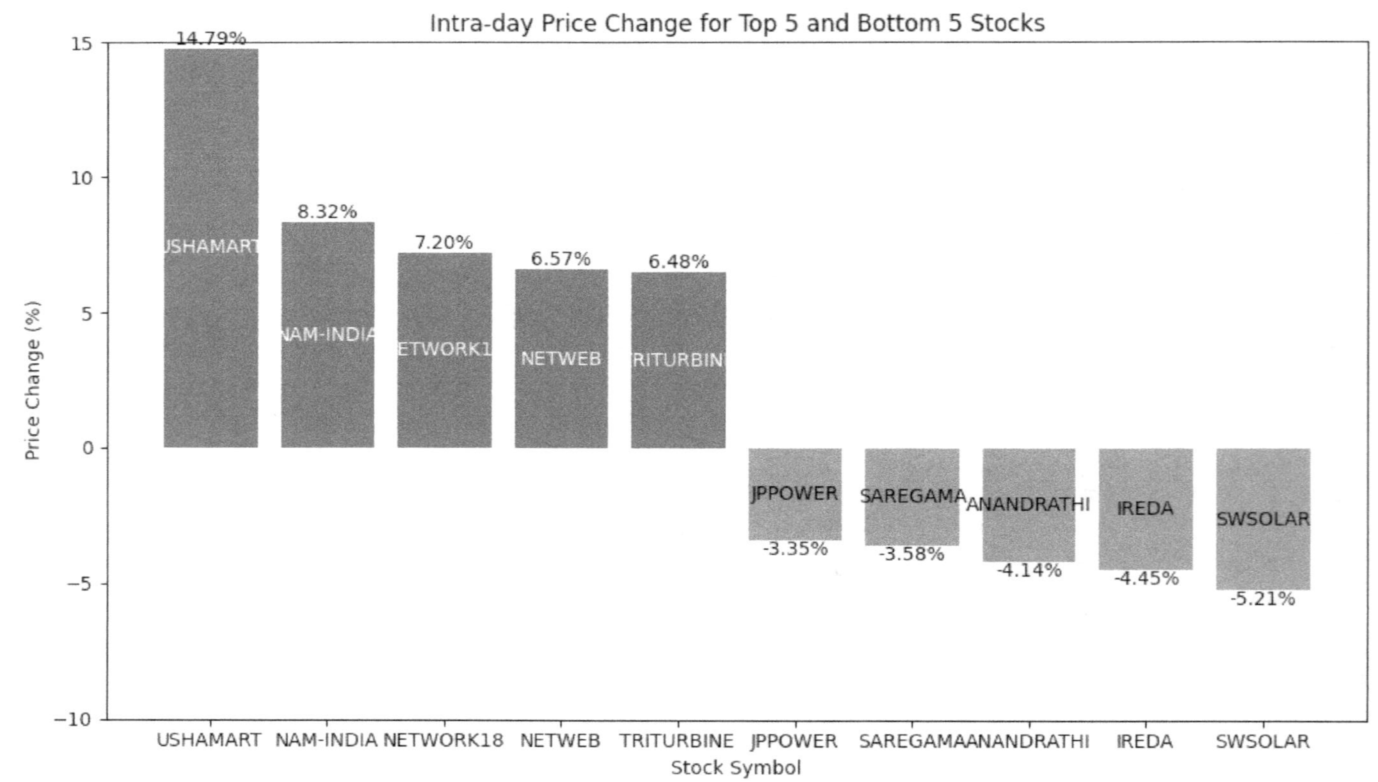


Intra-day Price Change for Top 5 and Bottom 5 Stocks
Price Change (%)
Stock Symbol
USHAMART
NAM-INDIA
NETWORK18
NETWEB
TRITURBINE
JPPOWER
SAREGAMA
ANANDRATHI
IREDA
SWSOLAR
14.79%
8.32%
7.20%
6.57%
6.48%
-3.35%
-3.58%
-4.14%
-4.45%
-5.21%
15
10
5
0
-5
-10

## 17. Haircut data with tkinter module

### 17.1 What is haircut?

Haircut of an equity refers the collateral margin money confiscated during pledging that specific scrip while initiating a position by shorting stocks or indices in derivative markets. It depends on many factors and is an imperative tool to measure the real appreciation of an equity and is correlated by its haircut percent. Its weightage is updated by NSE (National Stock Exchange, India), on everyday via its prior performance and preset standards. This work briefs out the Python algorithm and the relevant coding to fetch the historical haircut data to assess the variations in the underlying value of an equity in terms of its capability to yield the margin for trading in stock derivatives, options or future writing. Specific emphasis is given for industrial chemical sector and their depreciation and appreciation correlation with reference to a specific time period. The code can be compiled and deployed to analyze six chemical industries shares over a period of nine years.

In futures & options trading (derivative market of NSE), haircut is used as a safeguard for the lender's interests in the event that the price falls. For instance, while pledging an equity of worth INR. 10 lakhs to a lender and if the price drops 5%, the lender will lose 5 % of the holding value. So, during pledging a share, haircut is intended to cover such depreciation risks. These risks include elements that might affect the collateral's value, if the lender desires to sell the security in the event of default.

LTP, beta, liquidity of the share, and its primary as well as secondary market value all affect a stock's haircut or share's haircut. The value of haircut percent is predicated by the NSE on daily basis for every listed stock, for the significant depreciation or on the event of default. It helps to assess the real-worth of a share not only for lenders but also for investors. It depends on many factors such as price volatility, consistency over rate of return, beta value, dividend yield, earnings per share (EPS), stakeholder's pledge, promoter's holding, net debt per equity, Piotroski score, sectoral PE, volume as well as price fluctuations over the specific period etc.

It must be perceived that the collateral value of margin money for a share delivered on a trading day by pledging a share through specific depository participants should be utilized for writing CE or PE in stock or index option chains at different strike prices or shorting in future derivative markets. It cannot be utilized for purchasing a share or taking a long position in call or put of option chains or futures in current as well as future month expiries. This is because of the variation in the haircut value of a given share. Hence, heavyweight blue-chips are having relatively lower haircut with higher collateral margin, though the margin value is lower than the market values.

A haircut is also denoted as the market maker's spread. And the haircut percent and the collateral margin value often referred inconsistently for a share, but both reflects the money received for trading in derivative markets by pledging a share.

It must be mentioned that the mark to market (MTM) value for any short position will change day-to-day and hence the haircut percentage will be changed every day based on the prior closing price.

## 17.2 Methodology

The algorithm to fetch the haircut data and to assess the change in the value of a stock with time is based on Python coding. In this work by web scrapping from archives of NSE website, haircut data are fetched. Because by manual collection followed by analyzes of such data is cumbersome and time-consuming. By deploying .csv and numpy modules, the collected data can be analyzed to assess the real appreciation or depreciation of a scrip over the specific period.

## 17.3 Algorithm

Web scrapping and to fetching the scrip data is from NSE archives. It consists of the following five blocks:

1. Deploying tkinter module for graphical user interface of period selection

2. Validating the user input data for a specific scrip in str() format.

3. URL formatting based on the specified date for web scrapping.

4. Importing the request module to fetch csv file from archives.

5. Analyses via .csv file writer and numpy data frame modules for the scrip.

numpy or panda's data frame modules are intentionally excluded with reference to non-programmer's perspective. Basic fetching the data is given in the code without exporting the data.

Hyperlink to the haircut data:

https://archives.nseindia.com/content/equities/APPSEC_COLLV AL_ddmmyyyy.csv                    (replace: ddmmyy)

For the date: 10-October-2024, the link is:

https://archives.nseindia.com/content/equities/APPSEC_COLLV AL_10102024.csv

**Algorithm to export the fetched data as .csv**

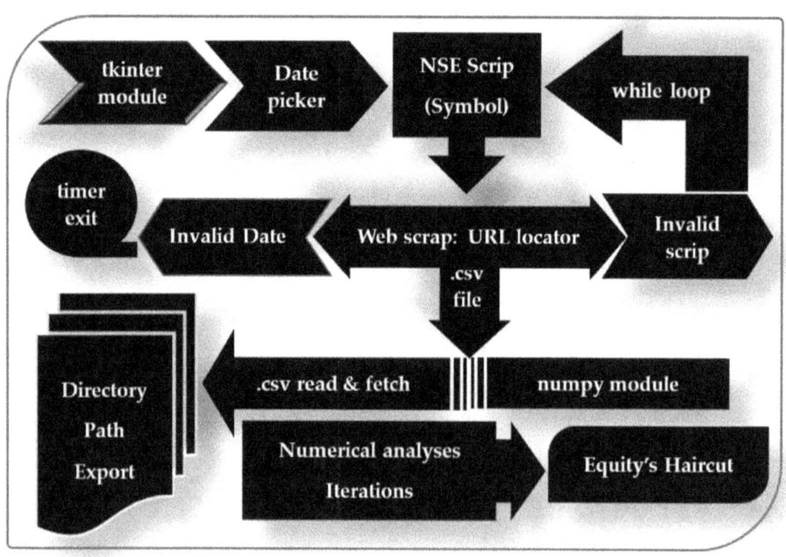

## Code

```python
eq = str(input("Enter the NSE symbol of the equity:    "))
import requests
import time as t
import webbrowser
import csv
def get_date():
    import tkinter as tk
    from tkinter import ttk
    from tkcalendar import Calendar, DateEntry

    def cal_done():
        top.withdraw()
        root.quit()

    root = tk.Tk()
    root.withdraw() # keep the root window from appearing

    top = tk.Toplevel(root)

    cal     =    Calendar(top,    font="Courier    14",
selectmode='day', year=2024, month=10, day=3)
    cal.pack(fill="both", expand=True)
    ttk.Button(top, text="ok", command=cal_done).pack()

    selected_date = None
    root.mainloop()
    return cal.selection_get()


try:
    date = []
    price = []
    haircut = []

    x = get_date()
    x=str(x)

    given_year = x.split('-')[0]
    given_year = given_year.replace("-", "")
    given_month = x.split('-')[1]
    given_month = given_month.replace("-", "")
    given_day = x.split('-')[2]
    given_day = given_day.replace("-", "")
```

```python
    given_year = str(given_year)
    given_month = str(given_month)
    given_day = str(given_day)
    date1 = given_day + "-" + given_month + "-" + given_year
    filename = date1 + '.csv'
    print ("")
    print("Selected equity is: ", eq)
    print("Selected  date  is:  "  +  given_day  +  "-"  +
given_month + "-" + given_year)

    required_date = (given_day + given_month + given_year
+'.csv')
    url                                                   =
'https://archives.nseindia.com/content/equities/APPSEC_CO
LLVAL_'
    req = requests.get(str(url)+ str(required_date))
    url_content = req.content
    file = open(eq +'.csv','wb') # keep as .csv file
    file.write(url_content)
    file.close()
    with open(eq +'.csv') as file:
        x = csv.reader(file)
        for row in x:
            if row[1] == eq:
                print("Haircut (%): ",  row[4])
                print("Price: ", row[3])
                date.append(date1)
                haircut.append(row[4])
                price.append(row[3])
                file.close      # to save the data

except IndexError:
    print ("Data not available, check the date and symbol")
    pass  # On error such as the date falls on holidays.
```

## Output

```
Enter the NSE symbol of the equity:   RELIANCE

Selected equity is:  RELIANCE
Selected date is: 11-10-2024
Haircut (%):  9
Price:  2742.1
```

```
Enter the NSE symbol of the equity:    ADANIGREEN

Selected equity is:  ADANIGREEN
Selected date is: 11-10-2024
Haircut (%):  20.72
Price:  1780.5
```

### tkcalendar interface

```
tk                                              —   □   ✕
◄  October  ►                          ◄ 2024 ►
     Mon  Tue  Wed  Thu  Fri  Sat  Sun
40    30   1    2    3    4    5    6
41    7    8    9    10   11   12   13
42    14   15   16   17   18   19   20
43    21   22   23   24   25   26   27
44    28   29   30   31   1    2    3
45    4    5    6    7    8    9    10
                     ok
```

Note

     tkcalendar interface is given to avoid the selection of date, which is falling on a holiday. If a holiday is selected, no data will be fetched. To implement the code, tkinter modules and tkcalendar should be installed and updated.

     Haircut Data for all equities at the selected date is stored as .csv. From this .csv file, data for the selected equity is fetched.

     Like this, other data such VaR (Value at risk), Deliverable quantity (%) etc., for an equity or a mutual fund at the selected date can also be fetched.

## 18. Download links for Python codes

All these Python codes can be downloaded from the following home page: https://www.enote.page/

**Download links to individual programs:**

https://www.enote.page/2024/10/Python-Coding-Stock-Market-Data.html

# Python codes to fetch & analyze NSE stock market data

## 19. Fetching the Bank NIFTY option chain data

### 19.1 Correlating the change in Open Interest (OI) and Price

Open interest is an important information for option traders, specifically to predict the trend. Either decrease or increase in OI as well LTP for the given strike price can be used to predict the trend. From the option chain data, based on change in OI (%) as well as price (%) values either for index or for equity, the price trend may be correlated as:

**Price trend with LTP and OI**

| Price | Open Interest | Price trend |
|---|---|---|
| Increase | Increase | Increase<br>(More buyers & long build-up) |
| Increase | Decrease | Increase<br>(Short positions covering) |
| Decrease | Increase | Decrease<br>(Short positions build-up) |
| Decrease | Decrease | Decrease<br>(Long unwinding, Buyers become sellers) |

And it must be emphasized that such data is more useful for option chain traders specifically strike prices which are near to underlying price that few strike prices near the 'In the Money'

(ITM) or the 'Out of the Money' (OTM) option chain. Far deep ITM or OTM values in the option chain are having less impact in change in OI or LTP.

## 19.2 JSON link for Bank NIFTY index option chain data

Steps are similar to equity, but the webpage source should be inspected with the desired Index.

In the home page (https://www.nseindia.com/), search for the desired Index, for example, Bank NIFTY.

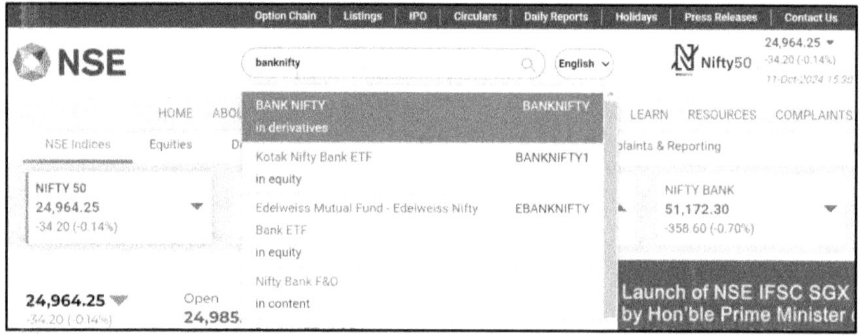

Then select Option Chain tab

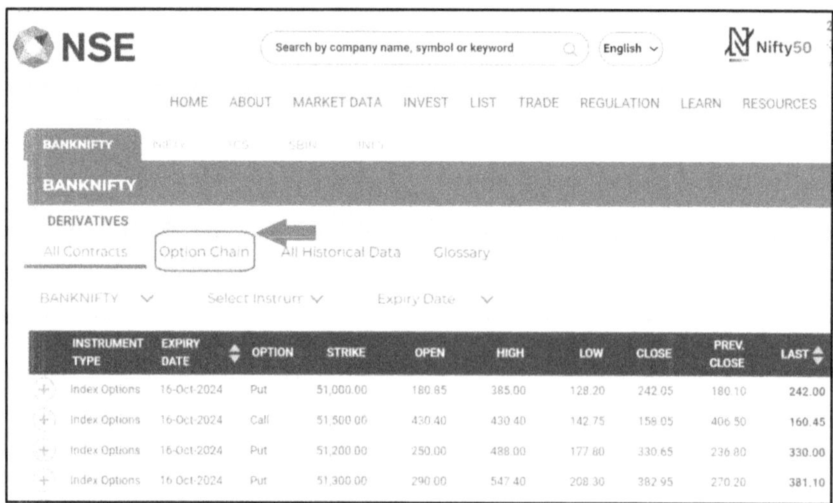

Now right click and then Inspect.

Then select Network and Refresh the Page (CTRL+R).

Ensure Option Chain tab is selected.

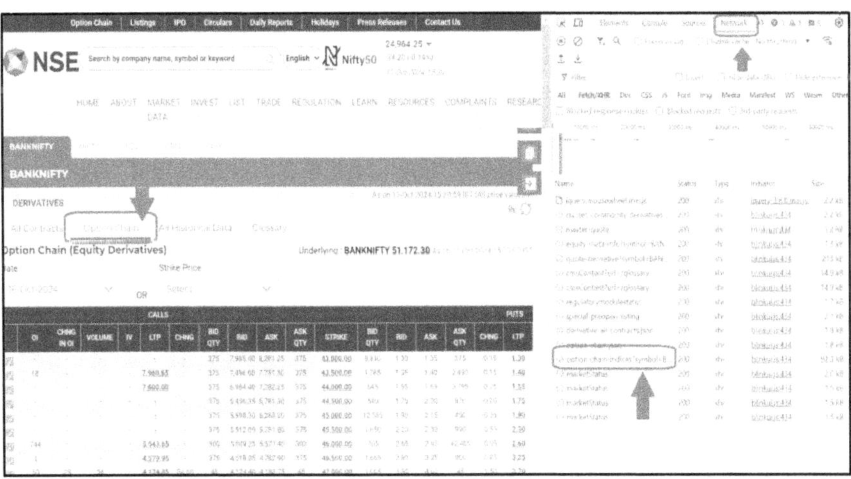

Then find the required JSON link, by using suitable JSON beautifier. Check for the required data such OI, LTP and IV etc.

The JSON link for the Bank NIFTY is:

https://www.nseindia.com/api/option-chain-indices?symbol=BANKNIFTY

The JSON link for the NIFTY is:

https://www.nseindia.com/api/option-chain-indices?symbol=NIFTY

The JSON link for the HDFC BANK (equity) is:

https://www.nseindia.com/api/option-chain-equities?symbol=HDFCBANK

By this same way, JSON link for all indices as well as equities can be obtained. It must be emphasized that, this JSON will be periodically updated in live market hours.

To avoid the IP blocking for multiple requests by NSE and other errors, it is advisable to download the JSON file in the local directory with the extension. json.

**19.3 Fetching the required data for options trading**

Following code demonstrates fetching the following essential data in reference to option traders' perspective.

1. Few Strike prices data for CE as well as PE nearer to Underlying Price (near ATM, OTM and ITM to Underlying Price).

2. OI

3. Change in OI (%)

4. LTP

5. Change in LTP (%)

Following code fetches the Bank NIFTY option chain data for CE and PE, with 500 points below and above to the Underlying price of the Strike prices and the Underlying Price is 51172.30 as on 11-Oct-2024.


## Code

```python
import requests
import csv

# Define the URL and headers
url       =       'https://www.nseindia.com/api/option-chain-
indices?symbol=BANKNIFTY'
headers = {
    'User-Agent': 'Mozilla/5.0 (Windows  NT  10.0;  Win64;
x64)      AppleWebKit/537.36      (KHTML,      like      Gecko)
Chrome/58.0.3029.110 Safari/537.3',
    'Accept-Language': 'en-US,en;q=0.9',
    'Referer': 'https://www.nseindia.com/',
    'Accept': 'application/json'
}

# Create a session and fetch the data
session = requests.Session()
session.get('https://www.nseindia.com',    headers=headers)
# Establish a session with NSE
response = session.get(url, headers=headers)

# Check for a successful response
if response.status_code == 200:
    data = response.json()
else:
    print(f"Failed    to    fetch    data.    Status    code:
{response.status_code}")
    exit()
```

```python
# Extract the recent expiry date and underlying value
recent_expiry_date = data['records']['expiryDates'][0]
underlying_value = data['records']['underlyingValue']

# Display the title and underlying price
print("Bank NIFTY")
print(f"Recent Expiry Date: {recent_expiry_date}")
print(f"Underlying Price: {underlying_value:.2f}")
print()

# Prepare lists for CE and PE data
ce_data = [["Strike Price", "OI", "OI change (%)", "LTP",
"LTP change(%)"]]
pe_data = [["Strike Price", "OI", "OI change (%)", "LTP",
"LTP change(%)"]]

# Filter and collect data for "CE" and "PE" around the
specified strike price range
for item in data['records']['data']:
    if item['expiryDate'] == recent_expiry_date:
        strike_price = item['strikePrice']
        # Check if the Strike price value is within +/- 500
of the Underlying value
        # Only fetching the data for strike prices lying
near to Underlying price
        if abs(underlying_value - strike_price) < 500:
            # Extract data for CE and PE
            ce = item.get('CE', {})
            pe = item.get('PE', {})

            # Append CE data if available
            if ce:
                ce_data.append([
                    strike_price,
                    round(ce.get('openInterest', 0), 2),
                    round(ce.get('pchangeinOpenInterest',
0), 2),
                    round(ce.get('lastPrice', 0), 2),
                    round(ce.get('pChange', 0), 2)
                ])

            # Append PE data if available
            if pe:
                pe_data.append([
```

```python
                        strike_price,
                        round(pe.get('openInterest', 0), 2),
                        round(pe.get('pchangeinOpenInterest',
0), 2),
                        round(pe.get('lastPrice', 0), 2),
                        round(pe.get('pChange', 0), 2)
                ])

# Display the CE and PE data
print("CE data")
for row in ce_data:
    print(f"{row[0]:<15}    {row[1]:<10}    {row[2]:<20} {row[3]:<10} {row[4]}")

print("\nPE data")
for row in pe_data:
    print(f"{row[0]:<15}    {row[1]:<10}    {row[2]:<20} {row[3]:<10} {row[4]}")

# Save data to CSV file
with open('Bank_NIFTY.csv', 'w', newline='') as file:
    writer = csv.writer(file)

    # Write underlying details
    writer.writerow(["Bank NIFTY"])
    writer.writerow([f"Recent        Expiry        Date: {recent_expiry_date}"])
    writer.writerow([f"Underlying                Price: {underlying_value:.2f}"])
    writer.writerow([])  # Add a blank row for spacing

    # Write CE data
    writer.writerow(["CE data"])
    writer.writerows(ce_data)

    # Add spacing between CE and PE data
    writer.writerow([])

    # Write PE data
    writer.writerow(["PE data"])
    writer.writerows(pe_data)

print("\nData has been saved to Bank_NIFTY.csv")
```

## Output

```
Bank NIFTY
Recent Expiry Date: 16-Oct-2024
Underlying Price: 51172.30

CE data
Strike Price    OI          OI change (%)          LTP         LTP change(%)
50700           5179        16.7                   596.7       -38.97
50800           9648        45.04                  531         -40.79
50900           13602       12.51                  459.8       -43.73
51000           78601       37.5                   397.35      -46.0
51100           41207       54.51                  340.45      -48.75
51200           80335       158.69                 287.9       -51.54
51300           69028       102.04                 241.95      -54.02
51400           66446       136.64                 196.9       -57.69
51500           148467      63.31                  160.45      -60.53
51600           81541       56.91                  128.85      -63.55

PE data
Strike Price    OI          OI change (%)          LTP         LTP change(%)
50700           27294       12.7                   145         19.59
50800           37282       33.53                  172.3       24.72
50900           30984       0.89                   206.7       30.49
51000           110679      -5.0                   242         34.37
51100           57213       8.01                   284.05      37.12
51200           50788       -18.42                 330         39.36
51300           33335       -25.83                 381.1       41.04
51400           29695       -38.68                 437.2       41.99
51500           51681       -30.46                 503         44.35
51600           24175       -19.53                 569.05      44.25

Data has been saved to Bank_NIFTY.csv
```

## 20. Fetching the NIFTY option chain data

This code illustrates the NIFTY option chain data and the algorithm is similar to the previous Bank NIFTY data fetching.

The JSON link for the NIFTY is:

https://www.nseindia.com/api/option-chain-indices?symbol=NIFTY

As already mentioned, all data fields from JSON are updated periodically and the most recent data can be fetched.

<u>**Code**</u>

```
import requests
import csv

# Define the URL and headers
url      =      'https://www.nseindia.com/api/option-chain-indices?symbol=NIFTY'
headers = {
    'User-Agent': 'Mozilla/5.0 (Windows  NT  10.0;  Win64;
x64)     AppleWebKit/537.36     (KHTML,     like     Gecko)
Chrome/58.0.3029.110 Safari/537.3',
    'Accept-Language': 'en-US,en;q=0.9',
    'Referer': 'https://www.nseindia.com/',
    'Accept': 'application/json'
}

# Create a session and fetch the data
session = requests.Session()
session.get('https://www.nseindia.com',   headers=headers)
# Establish a session with NSE
response = session.get(url, headers=headers)

# Check for a successful response
```

```python
if response.status_code == 200:
    data = response.json()
else:
    print(f"Failed    to    fetch    data.    Status    code:
{response.status_code}")
    exit()

# Extract the recent expiry date and underlying value
recent_expiry_date = data['records']['expiryDates'][0]
underlying_value = data['records']['underlyingValue']

# Display the title and underlying price
print("NIFTY")
print(f"Recent Expiry Date: {recent_expiry_date}")
print(f"Underlying Price: {underlying_value:.2f}")
print()

# Prepare lists for CE and PE data
ce_data = [["Strike Price", "OI", "OI change (%)", "LTP",
"LTP change(%)"]]
pe_data = [["Strike Price", "OI", "OI change (%)", "LTP",
"LTP change(%)"]]

# Filter and collect data for "CE" and "PE" around the
specified strike price range
for item in data['records']['data']:
    if item['expiryDate'] == recent_expiry_date:
        strike_price = item['strikePrice']
        # Check if the Strike price value is within +/- 200
of the Underlying value.
        # This value is changed.
        # Only fetching the data for strike prices lying
near to Underlying price.
        if abs(underlying_value - strike_price) < 200:
            # Extract data for CE and PE
            ce = item.get('CE', {})
            pe = item.get('PE', {})

            # Append CE data if available
            if ce:
                ce_data.append([
                    strike_price,
                    round(ce.get('openInterest', 0), 2),
                    round(ce.get('pchangeinOpenInterest',
0), 2),
```

```python
                        round(ce.get('lastPrice', 0), 2),
                        round(ce.get('pChange', 0), 2)
                ])

                # Append PE data if available
                if pe:
                    pe_data.append([
                        strike_price,
                        round(pe.get('openInterest', 0), 2),
                        round(pe.get('pchangeinOpenInterest',
0), 2),
                        round(pe.get('lastPrice', 0), 2),
                        round(pe.get('pChange', 0), 2)
                ])

# Display the CE and PE data
print("CE data")
for row in ce_data:
    print(f"{row[0]:<15}     {row[1]:<10}     {row[2]:<20}
{row[3]:<10} {row[4]}")

print("\nPE data")
for row in pe_data:
    print(f"{row[0]:<15}     {row[1]:<10}     {row[2]:<20}
{row[3]:<10} {row[4]}")

# Save data to CSV file
with open('NIFTY.csv', 'w', newline='') as file:
    writer = csv.writer(file)

    # Write underlying details
    writer.writerow(["NIFTY"])
    writer.writerow([f"Recent          Expiry          Date:
{recent_expiry_date}"])
    writer.writerow([f"Underlying                      Price:
{underlying_value:.2f}"])
    writer.writerow([])  # Add a blank row for spacing

    # Write CE data
    writer.writerow(["CE data"])
    writer.writerows(ce_data)

    # Add spacing between CE and PE data
    writer.writerow([])
```

```python
    # Write PE data
    writer.writerow(["PE data"])
    writer.writerows(pe_data)

print("\nData has been saved to NIFTY.csv")
```

## **Output**

```
NIFTY
Recent Expiry Date: 17-Oct-2024
Underlying Price: 24971.30

CE data
Strike Price    OI           OI change (%)        LTP        LTP change(%)
24800           26763        15.91                181.6      -30.19
24850           11417        28.35                141.55     -35.57
24900           66343        78.99                105        -41.84
24950           80648        89.11                74         -48.68
25000           320468       70.71                49.4       -56.49
25050           180308       61.43                31.3       -64.31
25100           355361       30.29                20.2       -69.74
25150           198791       32.57                13.1       -73.45

PE data
Strike Price    OI           OI change (%)        LTP        LTP change(%)
24800           215579       97.52                16.6       -28.29
24850           86785        34.81                25.8       -17.04
24900           168273       39.96                40.4       -5.28
24950           121037       65.01                58.55      2.72
25000           217169       -8.17                85.5       12.06
25050           43152        -43.16               116        16.47
25100           74857        -33.26               154        20.08
25150           28126        -34.57               197.85     22.93

Data has been saved to NIFTY.csv
```

## 21. Fetching the option chain data for equities

This code illustrates how to fetch the option chain data for the equities and the algorithm is similar to the previously explained Bank NIFTY as well as NIFTY data fetching. But it must be noted that Index options are having weekly as well as monthly expiries whereas stock options are having only monthly expiries.

Following code is based on the equity HDFC Bank and the JSON link for the HDFC Bank is:

https://www.nseindia.com/api/option-chain-equities?symbol=HDFCBANK

It must be emphasized that to get a few strike price values of ATM, ITM and OTM around the underlying prices, the difference between these two values should be selected accordingly. It differs from stock to stock and in this case it is take as 50.

### Code

```python
import requests
import csv

# Define the URL and headers
url     =     'https://www.nseindia.com/api/option-chain-equities?symbol=HDFCBANK'
headers = {
    'User-Agent': 'Mozilla/5.0 (Windows  NT  10.0;  Win64;
x64)      AppleWebKit/537.36      (KHTML,      like      Gecko)
Chrome/58.0.3029.110 Safari/537.3',
    'Accept-Language': 'en-US,en;q=0.9',
```

```python
    'Referer': 'https://www.nseindia.com/',
    'Accept': 'application/json'
}

# Create a session and fetch the data
session = requests.Session()
session.get('https://www.nseindia.com',    headers=headers)
# Establish a session with NSE
response = session.get(url, headers=headers)

# Check for a successful response
if response.status_code == 200:
    data = response.json()
else:
    print(f"Failed    to    fetch    data.    Status    code:
{response.status_code}")
    exit()

# Extract the recent expiry date and underlying value
recent_expiry_date = data['records']['expiryDates'][0]
underlying_value = data['records']['underlyingValue']

# Display the title and underlying price
print("HDFCBANK")
print(f"Recent Expiry Date: {recent_expiry_date}")
print(f"Underlying Price: {underlying_value:.2f}")
print()

# Prepare lists for CE and PE data
ce_data = [["Strike Price", "OI", "OI change (%)", "LTP",
"LTP change(%)"]]
pe_data = [["Strike Price", "OI", "OI change (%)", "LTP",
"LTP change(%)"]]

# Filter and collect data for "CE" and "PE" around the
specified strike price range
for item in data['records']['data']:
    if item['expiryDate'] == recent_expiry_date:
        strike_price = item['strikePrice']
        # Check if the Strike price value is within +/- 50
of the Underlying value.
        # This value is changed.
        # Only fetching the data for strike prices lying
near to Underlying price.
        if abs(underlying_value - strike_price) < 50:
```

```python
            # Extract data for CE and PE
            ce = item.get('CE', {})
            pe = item.get('PE', {})

            # Append CE data if available
            if ce:
                ce_data.append([
                    strike_price,
                    round(ce.get('openInterest', 0), 2),
                    round(ce.get('pchangeinOpenInterest', 0), 2),
                    round(ce.get('lastPrice', 0), 2),
                    round(ce.get('pChange', 0), 2)
                ])

            # Append PE data if available
            if pe:
                pe_data.append([
                    strike_price,
                    round(pe.get('openInterest', 0), 2),
                    round(pe.get('pchangeinOpenInterest', 0), 2),
                    round(pe.get('lastPrice', 0), 2),
                    round(pe.get('pChange', 0), 2)
                ])

# Display the CE and PE data
print("CE data")
for row in ce_data:
    print(f"{row[0]:<15}    {row[1]:<10}    {row[2]:<20} {row[3]:<10} {row[4]}")

print("\nPE data")
for row in pe_data:
    print(f"{row[0]:<15}    {row[1]:<10}    {row[2]:<20} {row[3]:<10} {row[4]}")

# Save data to CSV file
with open('HDFCBANK.csv', 'w', newline='') as file:
    writer = csv.writer(file)

    # Write underlying details
    writer.writerow(["HDFCBANK"])
    writer.writerow([f"Recent        Expiry        Date: {recent_expiry_date}"])
```

```python
    writer.writerow([f"Underlying                    Price:
{underlying_value:.2f}"])
    writer.writerow([])  # Add a blank row for spacing

    # Write CE data
    writer.writerow(["CE data"])
    writer.writerows(ce_data)

    # Add spacing between CE and PE data
    writer.writerow([])

    # Write PE data
    writer.writerow(["PE data"])
    writer.writerows(pe_data)

print("\nData has been saved to HDFCBANK.csv")
```

## Output

```
HDFCBANK
Recent Expiry Date: 31-Oct-2024
Underlying Price: 1700.45

CE data
Strike Price    OI          OI change (%)       LTP         LTP change(%)
1660            1978        -14.78              53.3        23.81
1670            758         -18.05              45.95       26.41
1680            1292        -44.31              38.45       27.32
1690            1349        -31.0               31.95       29.88
1700            9446        -5.83               26.05       29.28
1710            1990        25.79               20.85       30.31
1720            3526        21.38               16.6        29.69
1730            2937        -19.99              13.05       27.32
1740            2317        -5.27               10.2        22.16
1750            7696        13.28               8.05        19.26

PE data
Strike Price    OI          OI change (%)       LTP         LTP change(%)
1660            2113        -9.82               9.7         -35.33
1670            1592        21.43               12          -33.88
1680            1900        -7.45               14.6        -33.49
1690            1105        35.09               17.85       -32.89
1700            4942        8.66                21.8        -31.01
1710            883         65.36               26.75       -29.14
1720            1262        9.45                32.15       -27.1
1730            669         -7.47               39.35       -25.12
1740            488         0                   45.55       -23.51
1750            2100        69.22               54.4        -20.53

Data has been saved to HDFCBANK.csv
>>>
```

Based on the above code, it is possible to fetch various data for equities as well as index such as implied volatility (IV), traded volume, buy and sell quantity etc.

Like these, by identifying the required parameter's keyword, required data can be fetched, tabulated and can be analyzed. By running the module at regular intervals it is possible to get the updated data for such values.

# Index

## J



## K



## L



## M

<table>
<tr><td align="center">W</td><td></td><td align="center">Y</td></tr>
</table>